THE
AMERICAN BICYCLE

Jay Pridmore
and
Jim Hurd

Motorbooks International
Publishers & Wholesalers

First published in 1995 by Motorbooks
International Publishers & Wholesalers, PO Box 2,
729 Prospect Avenue, Osceola, WI 54020 USA

Motorbooks International books are also available
at discounts in bulk quantity for industrial or
sales-promotional use. For details write to Special
Sales Manager at the Publisher's address

Library of Congress Cataloging-in-Publication Data
Hurd, James.
    The American bicycle/James Hurd and Jay
    Pridmore.
        p. cm.
    Includes index.
ISBN 0-7603-0037-2 (hardback)
1. Bicycles—United States–History. I. Pridmore, Jay.
II. Title.
TL410.H87   1995
629.227'2'0973—dc20   95-38153

On the front cover: Schwinn's DX of 1941
featured a spring fork, tank, horn, headlight, and
other deluxe features. Balloon-tire cruisers like this
were industry mainstays from the 1930s through
the 1950s. This bike is a resident of the Bicycle
Museum of America in Chicago.

On the frontispiece: The simple grace of the high-
wheeler belied its disturbing tendency to launch
its rider over the handlebars.

On the title page: Bicycle mass production in the
early 1900s. The lessons learned by bicycle
manufacturers were applied by their successors in
the emerging auto industry.

On the back cover: *Top*: Perhaps the ultimate
sidewalk cruiser of all time, Schwinn's Black
Phantom incorporated all the most desired
features of the day in a package weighing only
slightly less than a comparably equipped Buick.
The Phantom pictured is from the Bicycle
Museum of America collection.
Bottom: Typical cycling garb of the day? Probably
not. When this photo was taken, Indian was
probably best known for its motorcycles, though
the company's roots were in bicycling.

Printed in Hong Kong

Contents

Acknowledgments

IN WRITING *THE AMERI-can Bicycle*, we tapped a variety of resources.

Our research depended in many ways on the collections and archives of the Bicycle Museum of America, Chicago, which was founded in 1993 and features as its nucleus the collection from the Schwinn History Center. We are grateful to the Schwinn family and Peter Davis, executive director of the museum, for their contributions to the industry as well as for their role in the creation of the museum.

Many photographs of bicycles displayed in the museum collection were made by Dennis Biela of Chicago whose skilled and faithful work yielded splendid results. Among additional photographers, Wendy Cragge of Marin County, California, has recorded the mountain-bike phenomenon for some two decades, and several action shots in the final chapter are hers. Others who provided pictures as well as indispensable slices of mountain-bike history are three of its earliest and most important pioneers: Joe Breeze, Gary Fisher, and Charlie Kelly. Carole Bauer of the Mountain Bike Hall of Fame in Crested Butte, Colorado, was an important source on the Rocky-Mountain roots of the sport, and also of photos from that museum's collection.

Craig Barrette, aka Gork, who is editor of *BMXer* magazine, the official publication of the American Bicycle Association, provided many shots of BMX racers in action as did Russ Okawa, an old BMX rider and now executive with Sachs bicycle components. Our section on Sting Rays depended in large part on conversations with Al Fritz, formerly of the Schwinn bicycle Company. *Low Rider* magazine also deserves our thanks.

For recumbent information, we spoke with Grant Bower of ATP/Vison, Gardner Martin of Easy Racers Dick Ryan of Ryan Recumbents, and Bob Bryant of *Recumbent Cyclist News*. To them, thanks and good luck.

In the 60s and 70s, there was a renaissance of lightweight and racing bicycles in the United States. In writing and illustrating that history, we had much help from Peter Rich of Velo-Sport Cyclery in Berkeley, California; George Koenig, former member of the legendary Pedali Alpini club; and John Finlay Scott, an early ten-speed devotee as well as early mountain biker. Rudy Schwinn told us stories about the advent of the Varsity. On the history of bicycle paths, Cathy Buckley Lewis of the Massachusetts Central Transportation Planning Staff was helpful.

Special thanks go to three leading bicycle people whose stories spanned many decades. Horace M. Huffman, Jr., is former president of the Huffy Corporation; Norman Clarke is former president of the Columbia Bicycle Company; and Phyllis Harmon is a stalwart of the League of American Wheelmen and provided us with wonderful photos of touring in the 40s. Neil Bailey loaned us a fine photo of his Huffman Safety Streamliner, a milestone cruiser of the 1930s.

Six-day racing was a fascinating story which was told to us in interviews with a number of the racers themselves, including Frank Brilando, Norman Hill, Bill Jacoby, and Jerry Rodman. Their mechanics were also central characters in these sometimes wild marathons, and those stories came from Bill Brennan and Oscar Wastyn, Jr. Jeff Gorman, owner of a bike shop in Kingston, Washington, was also helpful in reconstructing these episodes of bicycle history.

For stories of early racing, we depended in large measure on two books, *Hearts of Lions* by Peter Nye, and *Major Taylor* by Andrew Richie. Also important in these sections of our book were contributions from Vince Menci of the U.S. Bicycling Hall of Fame in Somerville, New Jersey, and Dale Ogden of the Indiana State Museum in Indianapolis, where the papers of Major Taylor now reside.

For early bicycle history, we were lucky to have had conversations with several people whose knowledge ran deep. Don Adams of the Henry Ford Museum, Dearborn, Michigan, was generous in his interpretations, as was Carl Burgwarde of the Burgwarde Bicycle Museum, Orchard Park, New York. Several members of The Wheelmen, a national organization for the preservation of pre-1917 bicycle history were also helpful: Bill Smith, Harold Cowell, Fred Fiske, David Gray, and Carl Wiedman.

Thanks also to the Kenosha County Historical Society, and staff members Dane Pollei and Beverly McCumber, for information about the successful transition of inventor-entrepreneur Thomas B. Jeffery from Rambler bicycles to automobiles, and to Vince Ruffalo, a Rambler enthusiast. The Carillon Historical Park Museum in Dayton, Ohio, supplied us with a photo of an old Wright Brothers-built Van Cleve.

David Herlihy and the Lallement Memorial Committee provided much information about the very first bicycles in America. Albert A. Pope, great grandson of the first bicycle magnate in the United States, was generous in providing a history of Colonel Albert A. Pope. Jim Langley, West Coast technical editor of *Bicycling* magazine, was most generous, particularly with his views of the bicycle industry's future.

There are many others to thank, Larry Bush, Harv Tromley, Paul Grimshaw, John William Roberts, Gary Woodward, Mike Bobis, Mark Mattei, Bob Harton, Rob Miller, Big Ed Druskas, Jim Owens, Les Wagonheim, Wes Pinchot, Robert C. Hurd, and Espernza Llamas.

We also thank the people at Motorbooks International, our editor Zack Miller, and company president, Tim Parker, for their patience and enthusiasm for this project.

We owe enormous debts to our wives, to Kim Coventry, whose support was as indispensable as it was cherished and to Toni Gordon, a partner whose belief in a dream helped infinitely to make it come true.

Among many others, Rick Podsiadlik deserves special recognition for his help in sifting through collections, locating valuable archives, and making important suggestions throughout the preparation of the text and illustrations. Rick is a true devotee of bicycles and helped immeasurably in making this a better book than it would have been otherwise.

To all, many thanks. We hope that our efforts prove worthy of your contributions.

—J.P and J.H.

Introduction

EVER SINCE COLONEL Albert Pope wandered into a small exhibit of English high-wheelers at the 1876 Centennial Exposition in Philadelphia, bicycles have provided a lens for many broad themes of American history. Pope promptly built a great new industry, and within a few years many minds throughout the country were focused on the problem of designing and building a better bicycle.

Socially, too, bicycles were a hand maiden of change. In the decade of the nation's first "bicycle boom," the Gay 90s, bicycles helped revolutionize American society. Workers who could afford the $50 or $100 needed to buy one had a new sense of mobility and freedom. Women unlaced their corsets and began pedaling around town unescorted.

As if to prove the power of the bicycle in these years, there was also stout resistance to it. Some preachers deplored "bicyclism," accusing cyclists, among other things, of competing with church on the Sabbath. And naturally conservatives looked askance at women in bloomers and on speedy two wheelers. But bicycles were not to be scuttled by Luddites.

It would be difficult and probably pointless to prove that bicycles caused social mobility or women's liberation. But the undeniable fact is that the invention accompanied those trends very closely. Thus, bicycle history touches many important, and often entertaining, aspects of American history.

Therein lies the charm and importance of the Bicycle Museum of America in Chicago, from which most of the illustrations in this book were drawn. The Museum, of which co-author Jim Hurd is co-founder and curator, possesses one of the world's most important collections of antique and classic bicycles, some 300 of them, and countless pieces of memorabilia, photographs, and archival material. The Bicycle Museum was founded in 1993 through the acquisition of several collections—including that of the Schwinn family. These collections were assembled by individuals passionate about the various human-powered machines that have populated American roads for more than a century.

There are many ways to enjoy the museum's collection and, we hope, this book. Modern-day inventors will appreciate the enormous variety of design in early bicycles and the decisions that led to standard forms. Business types will marvel at manufacturing empires that grew up around bicycles. Some early names in the bicycle business, such as Pierce, Rambler, even Ford, and the Wright Brothers, show that many two-wheel mechanics veered nicely into other industries. Still other visitors to the Museum enjoy fond memories of lightweight bicycles on the homefront before and during World War II.

But the consistent show stoppers of the museum—and perhaps of this book—are the "cruisers." These are the big, heavy, balloon-tire bikes that transformed the bicycle market in the 1930s and populated it with enthusiastic children for more than three decades. Quite naturally, these bikes are objects of intense nostalgia for many adults. Technically balloon-tire klunkers are not astonishing—though their introduction by Frank W. Schwinn is a wonderful story—but who can forget the pride of ownership in a Black Phantom or a Huffy Radiobike?

The American Bicycle is an attempt to capture and elaborate upon the wonderful past of the bicycle, from boneshaker to mountain bike. Some of the stories told, especially in the early chapters, have been told elsewhere. The empire-building of the first great bicycle magnate, Col. Pope, was chronicled even in his lifetime in important magazines such as Harper's Weekly. The story of racer Major Taylor, one of America's first great African-American athletes, has been neatly written as well in recent books by Andrew Ritchie and Peter Nye.

But other stories in our book come directly from the people who lived them. The bicycle renaissance of the 1960s was led in many ways by groups of eccentric kids who found ten-speed bicycles to be exotic and irresistible. Perhaps the most wonderful story of these is about a club called Pedali Alpini in Northern California. Its members were teenagers whose hero was the Italian, Fausto Coppi, and who learned to speak Italian and insisted on spaghetti at every meal. Their real-life story foreshadowed the movie *Breaking Away* by more than a decade.

And the story of mountain bikes, one of the last episodes of this book, was assembled through marvelous conversations with the people who invented them. Primarily they were long-haired teemagers from California who had a road racing club but loved nothing more than to park their ten-speeds and ride klunkers—mostly Schwinns—down mountain trails in Marin County. Based on the dimensions and durability of the old cruisers, they began designing and building new models for off-road use. They started in their garages, and a few of them became some of the most important bicycle entrepreneurs of the 1980s and 1990s.

All of this constitutes a sweeping history that has not been assembled previously all in one place. Like the museum, this book seeks to consolidate the stories, the nostalgia, and the technology into a single narrative, a framework that we humbly submit as a slice of American history. But perhaps a more important mission of both book and museum is the sense of enjoyment that bicycles instilled in Americans 100 years ago, and continue to instill today.

Bicycles may someday achieve the ambition of many designers and environmentalists as a truly important mode of transportation in the United States. Unfortunately, such is not the case today. The bicycle movement continues to encounter obstacles, such as our nation's abject dependence upon cars. But bicycles always have been a vehicle for enjoyment. If *The American Bicycle* has any underlying theme, it is that sense of serendipity, freedom, and fun.

—*Jay Pridmore, Chicago, July 1995*

Chapter One

Velocipedes and Boneshakers

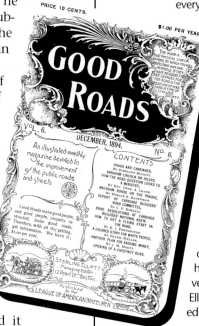

IN AN AGE OF MUCK-raking journalists and sensational headlines, an editor named Sterling Elliott stood out. In his profession, Elliott was decorous and usually polite in his magazine, the *League of American Wheelmen Bulletin*. He sometimes scolded racial prejudice, which was a problem in bicycle circles, and he revealed distinct impatience with sanctimonious preachers who railed from their pulpits on the evils of Sunday riding. But mostly he was restrained in his opinions.

Elliott did have a grievance, however, which he vented with some persistence. It was the subject of the history of the American bicycle. This was a reasonable issue for Elliott, as his readers, who numbered over 100,000 at the height of the publication's popularity, were mostly cycling devotees. Elliott believed that there was entirely too much being written on bicycle history, and much of it was myth and hokum. "We may expect," he wrote sardonically, "to see the subject, briefly treated, printed on the back of wedding invitations or run as a footnote to funeral notices."

In fact, the development of the bicycle in America was of more than average interest in the waning years of the nineteenth century. The country was in the midst of its first true "bicycle boom," which began in the early 1890s. Quite simply, no single technology had ever before overtaken society with so much force and enthusiasm. Bicycles got young people out of their insular neighborhoods. It got women—or many of them—out of their corsets. And it

RIGHT: Shire Boneshaker
J. Shire & Co., Detroit, Michigan
Late 1870s
The Shire was among the most advanced of boneshakers, though still a difficult machine for the purpose of common transportation. A large front wheel and a low saddle meant that a fast ride was possible, if only the rider could overcome the difficulties in pushing forward on the pedals while leaning back at a severe angle.

Good Roads was one of many cycling journals in the 1880s and 1890s. The strong editorial voice of Sterling Elliott raised this magazine, which later merged with the *Bulletin of the League of American Wheelmen*, to preeminence in the field and a circulation of well over 100,000. Besides printing travels pieces and humorous doggerel, Elliott raised the issue that burned among cyclists everywhere: the improvement of American roads. "The road is that physical sign or symbol by which you will understand any age or people," he declared on the magazine's cover. Good roads equated with civilized society. So did a strong community of cyclists, whose history was taken very seriously by Elliott and many other editors at this time.

created an enormous new industry with an output, by the middle of the decade, of at least 1.5 million bicycles yearly.

Many important Americans grew very interested in the bicycle. Politicians rode it to demonstrate their healthfulness and vitality. Mechanics tinkered endlessly with a technology that had room for improvement through lighter metals, better tires, fancier gearing, and other changes that were reported faithfully in the pages of technical magazines such as *Scientific American*. Industrialists built markets for bicycles at the same time as they also built some of the most advanced factories in the nation.

Before long, many of the people who helped develop the bicycle in America would turn their attention to ever more amazing machines, such as the automobile and the airplane. But prior to the proliferation of internal combustion engines, the bicycle was a force that changed society as it had rarely been changed before.

In some respects, bicycle history touched on many themes that fueled the American dream. There were stories of solitary inventors and their clumsy first efforts that made the public laugh. There were also visionary men, great capitalists, who stopped at nothing less than empires that they protected with continued innovation when they could, and with vicious patent battles when they could not. Meanwhile, young couples courted on bicycles, which provided them with an opportunity to escape the steady gaze of their small neighborhoods. Another effect of the bicycle was the growth of racing, which vaulted some young Americans to a level of fame that athletes had never achieved before.

Blacksmiths and Boneshakers

The advent of the bicycle, which represents a vital slice of American history, actually went back to Europe, to the streets of Paris and London and eccentric blacksmiths working on anvils. No one inventor, nor any one nation, can lay certain claim to the original bicycle. It was invented and reinvented in many places over a period of centuries. But as we study the bicycle's fascinating past and search for crucial turning points in its history, we might look squarely to southern New England. It was there that a man who may well have been the true in-

ventor of the modern bicycle demonstrated what was then a preposterous contraption. It was near Ansonia, Connecticut, that this inventor, one Pierre Lallement, drew notice not only for riding a distance of several miles, but for performing the first recorded "header," an inadvertent, head-first flight over handlebars into a culvert alongside a badly rutted road. Despite certain Europeans who were developing inventions that preceded the basic bicycle, Lallement's invention-and his ride and fall- were a definite milestone in bicycle history. And Americans ought to be proud that the event took place not in England or France but in America, a nation of undeniable ingenuity.

Lallement's header jumps well ahead of the story, however, which begins, depending upon one's imagination, in ancient times. Bicycle aficionados claim that there were suggestions of two-wheeled, muscle-propelled conveyances on the walls of Egyptian tombs and later in the frescoes of Pompeii. The existence of these images is debatable, and indeed, if anything like a bicycle did exist in antiquity, records of it were faint, and traces did not show up again for many centuries. Still, it is not surprising that the mechanical idea of the bicycle, simple and eminently logical, should appear over the course of history. It simply required thinkers of extraordinary scope, such as Leonardo da Vinci, to begin to put the pieces together, at least in the imagination. Leonardo, the quintessential Renaissance man, may well have touched on the possibility of such a labor-saving machine in the midst of developing his many other unbuilt inventions.

Something like a bicycle shows up in the most important set of Leonardo's surviving me-

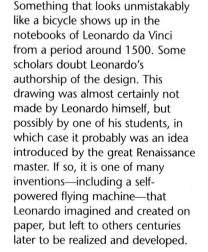

Something that looks unmistakably like a bicycle shows up in the notebooks of Leonardo da Vinci from a period around 1500. Some scholars doubt Leonardo's authorship of the design. This drawing was almost certainly not made by Leonardo himself, but possibly by one of his students, in which case it probably was an idea introduced by the great Renaissance master. If so, it is one of many inventions—including a self-powered flying machine—that Leonardo imagined and created on paper, but left to others centuries later to be realized and developed.

c. 1863 Michaux velocipede
Pierre Michaux et Cie., Paris, France
Pierre Michaux, a Parisian manufacturer of perambulators and other wheeled equipment, certainly built one of the world's first velocipedes. By putting cranks on the front axle and making a spectacle of himself on the street outside his shop, he was at least partly responsible for the velocipede craze that overtook Paris starting in 1863. But the very first inventor of such a vehicle may have been a more modest coach builder in Paris, Pierre Lallement, who also concocted a velocipede. At any rate, the Michaux velocipede is much like Lallement's, and for all the attention it commanded in France's most important city, it remains a key milestone in the development of the true bicycle.

vehicle. At any rate, the inventor quickly gained speed over a particularly steep part of the road.

"Exhilaration at his easy and rapid approach turned to consternation as his speed quickened to an uncontrollable rush down the slope," wrote Pratt. Ruts in the road and then a frightened team of horses conspired to force Lallement to swerve out of control. His front wheel turned crosswise to the line of his descent, with the inevitable result. The *veloce* stopped short, and its rider careened over the handlebars. .

Lallement, happily unhurt, quickly repaired to a local tavern, where two townsmen were discussing what they had just seen. They knew nothing of a French velocipede, and over glasses of ale they marveled about a creature with a snake-like body and a head like a devil. When Lallement overheard them, he smiled and confessed, "I was ze diable." He took the local gents outside to his machine to prove it.

Lallement's story, alas, did not end particularly well. In time, an entrepreneur named James Carroll was sufficiently impressed with the *veloce* to go into business with Lallement. The men applied for and received a patent. But they apparently lacked the capital to make much of the idea. Moreover, it is likely that the country roads of Connecticut were ill-suited to the primitive bicycle. Before too much more time passed, poor Lallement returned to Paris.

What he saw when he returned to France certainly must have produced mixed feelings in him. Paris streets were beginning to fill with *velocipedes a pedales*, which were being produced by a carriage-making concern called Michaux et Cie. and by others. They were even shown at the 1867 World's Fair, which was held in Paris. Lallement got back in the business. Some accounts have him working on his own and refining the machine so that each bicycle was designed according to the length of the rider's

RIGHT: 1869 Dexter velocipede
William van Anden,
Poughkeepsie, New York
Van Anden's patented velocipede included several improvements over previous models. One was the first free-wheeling drive, precursor of the coaster hub, with a ratchet-like device that allowed the cranks to remain motionless while the bicycle continued to roll. The brakes in van Anden's velocipede were particularly elegant—twisting the handlebars actuated a linkage with a friction plate against the rear wheel. Leather straps and springy iron frame also put the suspension of this boneshaker, however, primitive, well ahead of its time.

Velocipedomania, America's first short-lived bicycle boom, triggered substantial patent activity, such as the improvement represented by this drawing. Inventor Henry Laurence described "one or more adjustable auxiliary wheels or caster, so united and connected with the velocipede, and actuated by suitable mechanical contrivance and device, as to enable the person operating the velocipede to place the caster or auxiliary wheels in contact with the place or roadway." They were, in other words, training wheels.

legs. Others have Lallement working for Pierre Michaux who was turning out a production model that was affectionately known to English-speaking wags as the "boneshaker," for its metal-rimmed wheels and complete lack of suspension.

The French industry did not flourish, however. The Franco-Prussian War in 1870 put an end to bourgeois pastimes, and Michaux sold his company to people who sadly let it lapse. By now, of course, the bicycle idea no longer rose and fell with individual inventors. Already, some English shops were working on versions that sought to resolve some of the velocipede's obvious shortcomings. At the Crystal Palace in London, where new industrial goods were often introduced to the public, a machine called the Phantom was unveiled. It had a larger front wheel, producing a more efficient use of muscle power. It had a suspension saddle and solid rubber tires cemented to wooden rims.

It was around this time that the word "bicycle" came into use. It was a variation on the previously coined word for three-wheeled carriages with pedals and cranks being used in smart London circles: "tricycles." There was something about the patient English character that took to building better bicycles and eventually a new industry. By 1872, the first proper high-wheel bicycle, called the Ariel, was placed on the market. The Ariel was comparatively

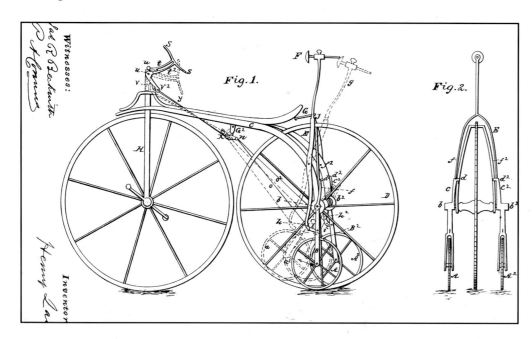

Witnesses: Fig.1. Fig.2. *Inventor*

RIGHT: c. 1870 Homemade high-wheeler American Blacksmiths with time on their hands fashioned high-wheeled bicycles several years before anything like an industry was born. They did not catch on at first, as most tradesmen and more than a few riders had bad memories of "velocipedomania" which came and went with a speed unknown to the old boneshakers themselves. Homemade high-wheelers were an improvement, but it would require wire spokes and some serious metallurgy before these bicycles would catch on in America.

Within a few years of Lallement's *veloce*, the Hanlon Brothers, American gymnasts and entertainers, used a velocipede in their act which became well-known and helped initiate a craze that became known as velocipedomania. Pictured here is another early bicycle, dated 1869, when the machine was appropriately called a "boneshaker," and the idea was still superior to the performance. Many carriage makers were getting into the business at this time, a decision that most regretted just a few years later when velocipedomania fell flat.

light, only 50 pounds, and more elegant than a French velocipede ever claimed to be. The high front wheel maximized the force of the pedaler (gears still being a thing of the future). The small back wheel provided balance while minimizing unneeded weight. With this basic design, the invention took on a life of its own. Within two years, some twenty English firms were involved in the manufacture and sale of high-wheelers, later called "penny-farthings," a name inspired by the relative size of the large wheel to the small one.

Meanwhile, America was having a bicycle surge of its own. It was triggered, in part, by the Hanlon Brothers, famous gymnasts who were headliners on the East Coast's pre-Vaudeville entertainment circuit. The Hanlons were trapeze artists, but more than the simple daredevils that they appeared to be on stage. As early as 1868 they successfully adapted their skills to the two-wheel velocipede. As they developed an improved machine for their act, they even got patents on several improvements to the basic Lallement machine. These included devices to adjust both the cranks and the seat to the size and comfort of the rider.

The next few years demonstrated just how quickly America could adopt a new mode of transportation. The respected *Scientific American* was quick to report on any and all developments of the velocipede—still of the "boneshaker" variety—and including the flying Hanlons' contributions. The magazine in these years was interested in the broad spectrum of science and technology, from cider making to early submarines, among which the bicycle was a machine with much promise, as the magazine reported in the 1860s:

To be sure the rider 'works his passage,' but the labor is less than that of walking, the time required to traverse a certain distance is not so much, while the exercise of the muscles is as healthful and invigorating. Practice with the machines has been carried so far that offers of competitive trials of speed between them and horses on the race course have been made.

As the bicycle became a common sight on the streets of many American cities, there was talk that Yankee ingenuity was just what the technology needed. *Harper's Weekly* acknowledged the French and English roots of the thing. But now it was here. "A number of professional inventors are now laboring to bring it to American completeness," the magazine wrote. Indeed, America popularized, commercialized, and even gospelized the bicycle. Riding schools called "velocinasiums" were established in cities to teach the art of riding, though "awkward movements, collisions, and shipwrecks" were endemic to the effort. Leading citizens even took up the sport. Charles Dana, publisher of the *New York Sun*, was no faddist, but he found it healthful and efficient, and he even called for an elevated path to run the length of Manhattan Island. Preacher Henry Ward Beecher was another aficionado. He declared that it was a worthwhile pastime and certainly appropriate for the Sabbath (though it must be noted that as time passed, the debate on this point would grow sharp).

The early American bicycle even rated its own periodical, the *Velocipedist*. "The two-wheeler

c. 1870 Ariel
Starley & Smith, Coventry, England
The Ariel was the most important early high-wheeler partly because of James Starley's "tension lever" wheels, with a spoke system that could be tightened by levers and wing nuts. The Ariel is remembered as the first production high-wheeled bicycle in England, and it was featured prominently at the Centennial Exposition in Philadelphia in 1876. When the American cyclists could only import bicycles, the Ariel was the best and most popular machine for those who dared ride such a thing.

and promising business, such that it changed its name to "Coventry Machinists' Company." Among engineers who participated in this transition was one James Starley, who became the leading bicycle maker of his generation.

To Starley goes the credit for a whole series of basic technological improvements that led to the modern bicycle. Early on, he devised techniques for making steel tubing that was light and yet strong enough to be suitable for bicycles. Later, as the front wheel of the standard bicycle grew larger and resulted in the penny-farthing, Starley invented the "lever-tension" wheel, with metal rods attached between hub and rim. When these rods were tightened, the hub turned slightly, increasing the tension on all spokes in one simple movement. It was an important advance in bicycle technology.

The lever-tension wheel was the major advance that led to the Ariel, which in 1872 became the first high-wheeler to reach the production stage. The Ariel also featured a hand brake for its small rear wheel and a saddle perched on a leaf spring, all providing a measure of comfort previously unknown to cyclists. The Ariel was a handsome machine, especially compared to the boneshakers of a decade before. Nevertheless, Starley's bicycle and other high-wheelers looked treacherous to Americans when they were first shown in Philadelphia. Reports from excitable journalists in this country were that death was a distinct possibility every time a rider climbed aboard.

There was one visitor to the Centennial Exposition, however, who took objective note of the English exhibit. Colonel Albert A. Pope, a successful industrialist from Boston, was fond

The American Championship Races at Springfield, Massachussetts, brought out the latest models by the manufacturers and the best riders that they could hire, often with cash on an under-the-table basis. Here the high-wheelers are primarily of the Columbia and Victor style, with the small wheel to the rear. Also represented in this picture, taken at the 1886 event, were high-wheelers with the balancing wheel in front, as introduced that year by the Smith Manufacturing Company of Smithville, New Jersey.

RIGHT: c. 1880 Facile
Ellis and Co., London, England
Another English version of an early safety bicycle, the Facile did what bicycle designers the world over were attempting to do. It made the drive wheel smaller, improved power transfer with levers, and moved the center of gravity back. The result was a safer bicycle that began to appeal to a more mainstream market and inspired other designers to keep working on it.

of new ideas, and the high-wheeler certainly looked like one. As he watched hired riders dazzling crowds in Philadelphia, Pope was impressed, but he quickly cautioned himself. He had seen high-wheeled bicycles in Boston, and they were ridden by eccentrics, he told a friend. "One must be an acrobat or a gymnast to ride such a steed," he reportedly said. Still, Pope returned to the English exhibit for another look, then another, and the more he looked at the bicycle, the more he imagined the roads of American cities and towns filled with them.

The exhibitors at Philadelphia had done little to emphasize the practicality of the bicycle. There were fewer than a dozen models on view, and some drew attention because they were stark oddities. One was an eighty-four-inch, high-wheel monster that did nothing to quell fears that bicycling might be a hazardous activity. Another was the unlikeliest of contraptions, a three wheeler called a "dogcycle" that was driven by the power of two large canines inside the two outer wheels. Despite these anomalies, Pope remained curious about what he had seen, which required substantial faith on his part, for the boneshakers of a decade before were still a bad memory for many American businessmen. Quite a few lost money trying to cash in on the nation's first brush with velocipedomania, and a larger number had dropped $100 or more on a boneshaking two wheeler that was now in permanent storage. On the way back to Boston, Pope's traveling companions were quick to say that the bicycle was neither practical nor desirable. Pope himself did not press the subject at that time.

The story did not end, however. As Pope continued to daydream about bicycles and weigh the pros and cons, another Bostonian, architect Frank W. Weston, was already making moves to eliminate doubt. Weston was born in

Attorneys—and Pratt in particular—became intimately familiar with another important aspect of the bicycle industry in those years. This was the almost endless round of patent suits waged among bicycle makers both big and small. Indeed, one of Col. Pope's earliest tactics was to seek and purchase any outstanding patents on the bicycle. The first and most important of these was the 1866 patent for Lallement's velocipede, which covered the most basic crank-and-pedal action. Pope's scheme to purchase, and later to enforce, the Lallement patent is one of the more revealing episodes of the early American bicycle industry.

LEFT: Many of the 150 wheelmen assembled at the first meeting of the League of American Wheelmen at Newport, Rhode Island, gathered for this photo May 30, 1880. No. "10" at the right, is Charles Pratt who was Albert Pope's attorney and prime organizer of the L.A.W. Pratt's book *The American Bicycler* was written in 1879, and it explained the basics of cycling, including the organization of bicycle clubs with uniforms, buglers, and other regalia in the interest of discipline and pride.

they were a force to be reckoned with. Together they would fight the anti-bicycle backlash, waged by horse-drawn carriage drivers, which was pushing for laws against wheels on public thoroughfares.

Wheelmen took to heart the words of their leader Charles Pratt. In his book he called the horse "a blindly cherished obstacle" to human and social progress. He later referred to the bicycle, rather archly, as being "like a bundle of sensitive nerves; it is beneath its rider like a thing of life, without the resistance and uncertainty of an uncontrolled will."

With Pope's money and Pratt's prose, the L.A.W. brought many issues of interest to cyclists to the center of public attention. The most rancorous debate of this sort took place in 1881, when Central Park in New York City was officially closed to cyclists. Indeed, there were anti-bicycle reactionaries aplenty to cause such a law to be passed. "If the bicycle was a great public convenience," wrote one bicycle opponent in the *New York Daily Graphic*, "there would be good reason to compel owners of horses to run the risk of being killed, but the bicycle is a toy at best . . ." Reports from wheelmen were nothing if not memorable. As one wrote: "Mr. Scott [a prominent bicycle opponent in New York] can congratulate himself that no law exists prohibiting idiots from entering Central Park, for if it did, Mr. Scott's personal knowledge of the park, would just about equal his acquaintance with the unexplored portions of Africa." With Pope himself pumping thousands of dollars into the effort, the prohibition of bicycles in the park was repealed.

"When we were boys together"
Sincerely yours,
HARRY T. HEARSEY,
Indianapolis, Ind.

The story began around 1880, when the Lallement patent was half-owned by the bicycle firm of Richardson & McKee, a small maker during the short-lived velocipedomania of more than a decade before. Richardson & McKee was no longer building bicycles, but it was deriving some income from its half of the patent through a royalty paid by the Boston firm of Cunningham & Heath, which was importing English high-wheelers with moderate success. While Pope himself was paying no li-

The League of American Wheelmen chapter in Indianapolis in 1887 was a well-heeled group that often made a proud spectacle of themselves in public places. In this 1887 photograph we see that most club members were fashionable, modern gentlemen on relatively late-model high-wheelers. The fellows on the wood-wheeled boneshakers in front would have been considered the antiquarians of the group.

censing fee at this time, he still believed it was in his interest to own the Lallement patent. To do so, he set out on a somewhat devious plan.

Pope first went to Richardson & McKee and made an offer for its half-interest in the patent—

an offer of somewhat more, he was sure, than it was worth. Pope reasoned that his offer would be accepted because, if they were at all clever, Richardson & McKee would figure that it could then simply take the proceeds of that sale and

PREVIOUS PAGE: 1884–1885 Kangaroo Hillman, Herbert & Cooper, Coventry, England

The Kangaroo had a short, two-year lifespan, but it stands as a clear milestone in the development of a safety bicycle powered by a chain drive. This device reduced the size of the front wheel to 36 inches and actually increased power over traditional high-wheelers—gear ratio was 2 to 1. A 100-mile record of seven hours, eleven minutes, and ten seconds was set on a Kangaroo, which inspired a brisk export trade to America. But it was eclipsed late in 1885 by the Rover, which had a rear drive wheel, was more comfortable, and shaved four minutes and 54 seconds off the 100-mile record.

RIGHT: The Columbia Light Roadster Safety, which was introduced in 1887, was the Pope Manufacturing Company's first safety bicycle. State-of-the-art at the time, it had solid-rubber tires, a skip-tooth chain, and front suspension.

tables and milling rooms of the factories. The great advance in the safety bicycle—which was, in effect, the modern two-wheeler—was the innovation of gearing. The basic principle was that through the use of sprockets and chain, a bicycle could multiply the output of muscle power to the rear wheel. It was not a new idea; da Vinci had sketched chains and gears in his notebooks. Still, the concept went through a number of unwieldy versions before James Starley came up with the Rover, in 1886. When it arrived in America—looking much like bicycles would look for years to come—the Rover changed everything. The bicycling press was filled with news about this bicycle of two equal-size wheels. Big and small American bicycle companies set about finding a design like it for themselves.

The safety bicycle not only revolutionized the standard design of the industry, it also multiplied the market for bicycles by many times. People who would not think of riding a high-wheeler because of the fear of headers were now potential customers which prompted a new round of innovations. For example, manufacturers, found that the sloped front fork added to stability, and that joining the frame together with pivot points of various types provided the smooth ride that the high-wheeler could not.

America quickly produced many early versions of the safety frame. One of the more interesting ones was Overman's elliptical form, a "racquet frame," which was reinforced inside by spokes. Gormully & Jeffery produced a Rambler in 1888 with finely curved tubes, though not enough of them, and the model was prone to breakage. At last, by about 1890, the diamond frame was hit upon. No particular inventor was credited with this simple design, though it appeared earlier in England than in America. The diamond shape was eminently serviceable as a basic design. When seat, pedals, or handlebars begged for realignment, the adjustment normally required only small changes in the shape or dimensions of the diamond.

Perhaps the most important diamond frame asset was its ability to drop the crossbar low without sacrificing strength. Again, there is

1889 Victor Safety
Overman Wheel Co.,
Chicopee Falls, Massachusetts
Americans were quick to develop
the safety bicycle based on the
English Rover model. Overman's
version was one of the best. Its
catalogue description noted that the
machine "rendered a backward or
forward fall impossible." The Victor
also advanced the art with a spring
front fork and adjustable saddle,
cranks, and handlebars.

no record of the first designer to produce such
a frame. What is clear is that the "dropped
frame" brought an entirely new constituency to
cycling: women, whose traditional garb had
previously made cycling not just difficult but
impossible. The combination of drop frames

and women cyclists did not simply help to ig-
nite a bicycle boom of unforeseen proportions.
It also ushered in a revolution—the social liberation of women—that was one of the most important developments of the end of the old
century and the beginning of the new.

1888 Elliott Hickory
Sterling Elliott, Boston, Massachusetts
Elliott owned a prominent addressing-machine concern, but like many entrepreneurs of the age he was taken up by the excitement of bicycles. His contribution to the industry, alas, did not include a production model that sold widely. Elliott stressed the resilience and beauty of wood with a few lines of two-wheel poetry, noting that his bicycle . . .

> Is a thing of such unique construction,
> That to be admired needs but introduction . . .

Ultimately, Elliott was more a wordsmith than a bicycle manufacturer, and he is remembered mostly for his editorship of the *L.A.W. Bulletin*.

Chapter Three

The Bicycle Boom

EVERY ERA HAS AN INvention that defines it. The "Gay 90s" belonged to the bicycle. Bicycle technology exploded in this decade. At least one-third of all new patent applications at the U.S. Patent Office were bicycle related. Hundreds of manufacturing companies were established to make and sell bicycles and accessories to a seemingly insatiable market.

As prices became reachable for more people—under $100 for a machine of good quality—the invention and the industry had a profound impact on society. "As a social revolutionizer it never had an equal," wrote *Scientific American* in 1896. Young people suddenly had the means to pedal beyond their conservative neighborhoods. Working people got bicycles and were quickly riding alongside more wealthy wheelmen. Most important, perhaps, bicycles encouraged a generation of women to discard their corsets, try on new-styled bloomers, and take to the roads.

So pervasive was the bicycle in the '90s that it was quickly adopted as a symbol of the American spirit. "The bicycle is the most democratic of all vehicles," wrote Charles Pratt in his cycling bible, *The American Bicycler.* It was hard to argue. As bicycling clubs, most affiliated with the League of American Wheelmen, proliferated, doctors and lawyers became indistinguishable from tradesmen and shopkeepers when pedaling proudly. Clubs declared themselves to be strictly egalitarian, and to reinforce the

RIGHT: 1897 Old Hickory
Tonk Manufacturing Co.,
Chicago, Illinois
Several manufacturers made the case that wood absorbed vibration in ways that steel could not. Perhaps the most memorable of the wooden bicycles from the boom decade was Tonk's Old Hickory. If it was not the sturdiest, the smoothest, or even the most vibration-free bicycle on the road, there is little doubt that it was the most elegant, with ornamental lugs and a gracefully spare design. Its price, in both men's and ladies' models was $100 in a period when most prices were rapidly sinking to below $50.

With the industry booming at the time of the Spanish-American War of 1898, bicycle manufacturers had great hope for the cycle's military use. Some outfitted safety bicycles with machine guns, and others simply advertised their wares via images of soldierly virtue. At any rate, military bicycles were never a strategic success, though designers continued to try even years later when a folding bicycle was designed to be dropped along with paratroopers. It never flew.

In the decade of the bicycle boom, prices came down to make cycling accessible to nearly all. A number of different styles differentiated the safety bicycle; among them nothing was quite so impressive as a fine racing machine with dropped handlebars.

the *New York Herald*, which described the event as the "apotheosis of the wheel." Twelve thousand cyclists were reportedly involved, many of them swathed in American flags as they rode down Riverside Drive. Among the units rolling past the reviewing stand were contingents of policemen and regiments of the National Guard. Officers saluted dignitaries by holding their gleaming sabers aloft. A throng of as many as 100,000 New Yorkers cheered lustily and no doubt dreamt of owning bicycles themselves. Many soon would.

By 1892, when this photo of the St. Louis Cycling Club was taken, the safety bicycle had displaced the high-wheeler, and clubs were booming in many cities and towns across the country. Most riders still bumped along on hard rubber tires, though the "cushion" tire, a hollow rubber tube which preceded the pneumatic, was making its appearance, in evidence here on the bicycle leaning in from the right-hand side.

equality concept, members wore uniforms, elected officers from their ranks, and observed orderly discipline on the roads—or tried to, though their strange looks continued to spook horses they encountered on the road.

Bicycles added to the spectacle of parades down the avenues of the nation's cities. They were often included in Independence Day festivities, and bicyclists even staged grand public celebrations for no other reason than to make a spectacle of themselves. One such bicycle parade in 1896 was sponsored by

1893 Columbia Century
Pope Manufacturing Co.,
Hartford, Connecticut
Wheelmen and wheelwomen were
enthusiastically trying to ride
"centuries," or 100 miles in a day, at
this time. For customers who were
this serious about cycling, Pope
introduced the Century with
pneumatic tires and an "elliptical
sprocket." This was designed for
greatest power when the rider's leg
was at its most advantageous point.
This innovation did not catch on
widely at the time, but by the 1980s
Shimano was doing the same thing
much its "Biopace" chain ring.

OPPOSITE PAGE BOTTOM: The
Massachusetts Bicycle Club was
one of many cycling organizations
in Boston, which was the true
cradle of American cycling. Here
in 1902, members of the club
ready themselves for a Patriot's
Day event. Riders are properly
uniformed and in the good
company of family members
availing themselves of a more
ancient mode of transport.

Cyclomania

Mainstream patriots were not the only ones to adopt the new machine as their own. At the University of Chicago, bicycles were *de rigueur* for erudite professors and fashionable students. Whatever cachet the bicycle had carried in the high-wheeler days, the advent of the safety bicycle increased the sheer numbers of enthusiasts. It also made for some unlikely converts. During one of John D. Rockefeller's visits to Chicago—he was the University of Chicago's original and greatest benefactor—the oil tycoon toured campus on bicycle, with University President William Rainey Harper and an entourage of faculty members also astride. The event naturally reinforced cyclomania in academia. Competitions were staged to prove the superiority of one fraternity over another, for example, or for classics over physics, with opposing faculty members racing one another. There was even a call in Chicago for Harper to challenge Harvard President Charles W. Eliot. The brilliant (but portly) Harper demurred.

Excitement about cycling trickled down through the social strata with uncommon speed. The earliest class of New Yorkers to take up cycling, naturally, was the society set, with names like Gould, Vanderbilt, and Winthrop. So devoted were they that in winter they held "musical rides" in rented halls where men and women could pedal in circles to the music of a live orchestra. As bicycle prices continued to drop the market greatly expanded. Chinatown merchants put a bicycling school together and rapidly took to riding in their neighborhood. The Japanese community had the Rising Sun Cycle Club, which was distinguished for its exceptional discipline.

With their numbers increasing almost daily in the boom decade, bicyclists became an indispensable political constituency. In 1897, the New York mayoralty election included three bicycle riders among the four candidates running. The Tammany Hall political machine put up candidate Robert Van Wyck, who advanced so many pro-bicycle planks in his platform that some of the newspapers implied that he was overdoing the matter. The political machine even put out a daily cycling newspaper which covered the local cycling scene as well as promoting Van Wyck's candidacy. Wheelmen

votes or no, the Tammany machine prevailed, and it even kept a few promises. A street-cleaning brigade called the "White Wings" was given instructions to pay particular attention to any rubbish or obstruction that might throw a cyclist off his or her machine.

Mainstream politicians were not the only ones who sought favor through the noble two-wheeled steed. Cycling became a pastime of the members of the Socialist Labor Party as well, and they proved themselves willing to campaign and proselytize as they also enjoyed the fresh air and open spaces of the road. The socialists were anything but shy about wearing crisp uniforms with caps and ties of blazing "socialist red." They were a young and hearty group, and in 1898 they earned some public notice for a ride that began in Boston and wound through New England to New York City. Wherever they stopped, they distributed their leftist literature, hoping that the good will coming to cyclists everywhere in the Gay 90s would rub off, in some measure, on their cause as well.

If politics came naturally to the world of bicycles, it was nothing compared to the national enthusiasm for health. It was the good luck of the bicycle, or of those who sold them, that the machine was introduced in an era of health fads of every type, from sleeping porches to high-fiber cereals and therapeutic enemas. Almost instantaneously, the bicycle was adopted by many health theorists, although it was distrusted—and with equal passion—by many others.

At the very beginning, bicycling was naturally viewed as a travesty for good health. Collisions and headers were the most obvious threats to maintaining fitness. Before long, physicians began witnessing a variety of aches and pains reported by people riding hunched over ill-fitting bicycles. A particularly imaginative doctor began diagnosing a disorder termed "posterior dorsal curvature," or more prosaically "bicycle hump." Cycling also led to excessive thirst, which sometimes prompted overindulgence in beer and resulting gallstones. Early reports were that children in particular ought not ride, as the sport would certainly damage their nervous systems.

In time, and with the growing endorsements of enthusiasts, the healthful effects of cycling were emphasized. And a number of physi-

1890 Bronco
White Cycle Co.,
Westfield, Massachusetts
Another transitional safety bicycle, the Bronco did not represent an ideal design. The cranks were too far back, and the gear was too high, but it represented one of many steps (and missteps) toward the elegantly simple diamond frame that would become standard within a few years.

Head tags and name badges were hardly a trivial concern in the bicycle boom. In the crowded industry which was dependent upon yearly improvements and upgrades, brand loyalty was precious, as was evident from these carefully cast and finely detailed works of art. Later, when standardization became the rule among bicycles, different badges adorned different brands, but the screw holes were all in the same place so the trademark could be changed at a retailer's will. After 1899 when the boom ended, there were many more marks than there were makers.

cians, inspired by fees paid by Colonel Pope, began taking that side of the issue as well. Thus, it became known that cycling could "equalize matters in respect to the general size of the body," as one doctor said, suggesting that the pastime ought to be taken up by both the stout and the lean. Another physician reported that the bicycle was being used to good therapeutic effect in insane asylums; it calmed the inmates and concentrated their minds.

Sometimes ironically, it seemed like the bicycle industry and the anti-bicyclists were working hand in hand. For example, medical studies in the midst of the bicycle boom alleged that bicycling caused excessive vibration on the body, leading in many cases to a disorder called "nerve death." Manufacturers responded quick-

ly and often profitably. To alleviate vibration problems, for example, they devised and placed on the market many innovations for a smoother and less jarring ride.

Many makers of bicycle saddles introduced alternatives with the comfort of the perineum in mind. Air cushions, cane seats, and even hammock-like seats made of cord—all these innovations were in search of a formula that would minimize the most obvious, not to say insidious, strain that a long day of cycling placed on the human frame.

It was not long before another crucial innovation overtook the industry and was rapidly promoted in the name of health. This was the inflatable tire. In the early, high-wheel years, solid rubber was the material of choice:

1897 Carroll Gear-to-Gear
Thomas A. Carroll,
Philadelphia, Pennsylvania
The bicycle boom and the competition of many companies in the market in the 1890s inspired much innovation. The gear-to-gear had three sprockets—one attached to the crank, one to the rear-wheel hub, and the middle one to the chain stay and a small fork from the drop bar. Because it came toward the end of the boom and the beginning of the bicycle bust, it was not developed. The Gear-to-Gear remains an exotic machine that was, in fact, a good-working version of early bicycle-transmission technology.

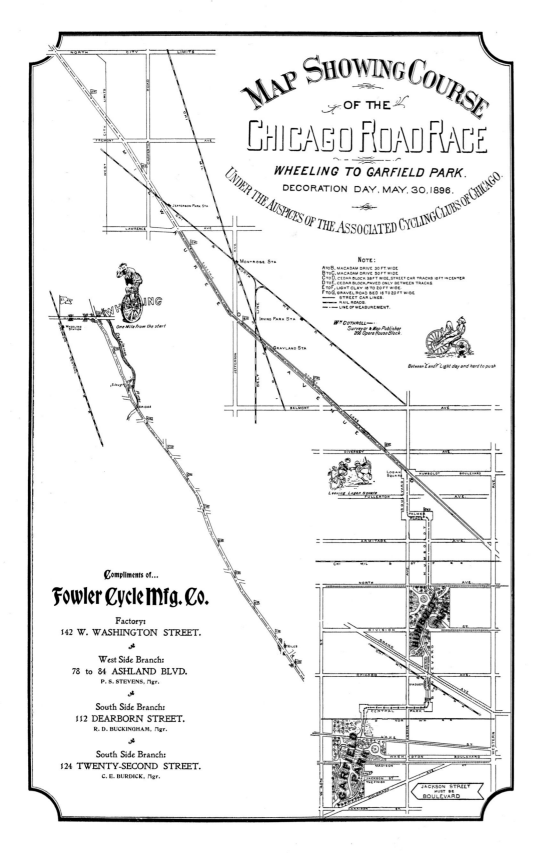

Compliments of...

Fowler Cycle Mfg. Co.

Factory:
142 W. WASHINGTON STREET.

West Side Branch:
78 to 84 ASHLAND BLVD.
P. S. STEVENS, Mgr.

South Side Branch:
112 DEARBORN STREET.
R. D. BUCKINGHAM, Mgr.

South Side Branch:
124 TWENTY-SECOND STREET.
C. E. BURDICK, Mgr.

hard, durable bands cemented to metal rims. Hard rubber was a necessary improvement over metal wheels, but it did not resolve the thrashing that riders endured on roads that were almost universally rough-and-tumble. With comfort and health as their objectives, engineers for Gormully & Jeffery in Chicago came out with a tire of solid rubber that extended beyond the rim and flattened somewhat when it encountered a small stone or other obstruction. Unfortunately, this idea sounded better than it performed, and it did not capture the market. "The flattened-out idea," as it was called, cushioned the ride somewhat, but slowed the rider considerably. While nerve death was an abstract concern in these days, experienced cyclists were most of all addicted to speed.

The ultimate replacement for rough-riding solid rubber originated in 1889, when a veterinary surgeon in Belfast, Ireland, by the name of John B. Dunlop devised the first pneumatic tire with an inner tube and an outer canvas shell. This was the beginning of the inflatable tire, which would quickly become standard not just for bicycles but for motorcycles and automobiles as well. Dunlop's tire was a godsend for cyclists in search of a smooth ride. Its efficacy was proved one day in Ireland when cyclist Bill Hume, a friend of Dunlop's, appeared at the starting line of a local road race with a pair of air-filled tires. Predictably, perhaps, the innovation inspired derision among other riders and spectators, as they looked slow and clumsy compared to sleek strips of hard rubber. Laughs were quickly silenced, however, when the race began and Hume shot out in front, winning by a convincing margin. The following year, the bicycle speed record for the mile sprint was "smashed all to smithereens," as one paper wrote, by a rider on a safety bicycle equipped with pneumatics. Time was 2 minutes, 26-4/5 seconds, and the news made Americans take notice. Dunlop's invention of a "double-tubed" tire was not adopted instantly in this country, but it was not long before variations on the air-filled tires were devised by several American bicycle makers.

Overman, for example, invented an "arched cushion" tire, which was hollow but not filled with pressurized air. Colonel Pope ini-

OPPOSITE PAGE: Road maps were a rarity in an age when transportation was left to public coaches and horse-drawn carriages. They proliferated in the years of the bicycle boom, and they constituted attractive advertising for smart bicycle manufacturers and retailers.

LEFT: Bicycle manufacturers employed all manner of shtick to attract attention. Here an actor in "Native American" garb at an 1897 carnival in Grand Rapids, Michigan, has been engaged to stand by a contraption using the power of two tandems to make a globe revolve. World bicycles were the original make of Arnold, Schwinn & Company, which was founded in 1895.

tially derided the Dunlop pneumatic, saying that it appeared notoriously liable to puncture, though he was probably concerned that Dr. Dunlop and not he who owned the patent for the idea. But a good businessman like Pope was anything but deaf to testimonies suggesting that hard rubber had a limited future. A member of the League of American Wheelmen from Highland Park, Illinois, claimed that his first set of pneumatic tires lasted a year, in which he rode over 3,000 miles in the U.S. and Great Britain. This cyclist was no bantam; he weighed in at 215 pounds, but he had no need for a sprung saddle, he wrote to the *L.A.W. Bulletin,* as long as he kept his tires relatively soft. Another ardent endorsement came from a W. C. Shallcross of Lansford, Pennsylvania. He wrote in the *Bulletin* that pneumatic tires, inflated "a trifle slack," alleviated the evil vibration of the road and actually made the machine run better and presumably faster.

By the early 1890s, Pope had his own version of the pneumatic, a single-tube inflatable tire popularly called the "hose pipe." Not many years later, Pope and others developed products that were simultaneously "puncture-proof" and "self-healing," meaning that thorns, tacks, tin cans, and glass were easily shed, but if something did penetrate the air chamber, the fabric of one of the nine or ten layers was reputed to close the breach. This was a dubious claim, but one which did, apparently, sell tires to cyclists, who were always eager for the latest technical advance.

Even as pneumatic tires were improved, the problem of excessive vibration continued to fill the pages of the cycling press. Some solutions focused on the loss of feeling in fingers and its etiology, stemming from the configuration and constitution of the handlebars. One L.A.W. member wrote that he had dealt with the problem by keeping his handlebars "in tune," which turned out to be a rather mysterious practice of sawing off an inch from both sides; the writer encouraged compatriots to try their own experiments in this vein. The industry also sought to introduce accessories that might achieve anti-vibration and some tidy profits at the same time. Cork and leather grips were sold, and some of them had ornate metal inlays. From England came "ram's horn" bars, which spiraled several times between the stem and the end, and were considered for a while to

be a serious guard against insidious nerve death.

Perhaps the boldest, if not the most convincing, case made for neutralizing bicycle vibration came from a few manufacturers who built machines primarily of hickory. The Elliott Hickory Bicycle Company was the brashest in claiming that wood was the choice material for bicycles and that steel was but a poor substitute. Sterling Elliott, ultimately the dean of cycling editors, started in the bicycle field as a manufacturer, and advertised archly that it was not for nothing that the great carriage makers eschewed steel. "Attempts to supersede timber for wheel construction have been as futile as they are numerous," Elliott's ad declared. This argument did not hold well among bicycle buyers, however. The Elliott Hickory made but a small impact in the market, and Elliot himself is best remembered as a pundit, not a capitalist, of note.

A Chicago firm, Tonk Manufacturing, also attempted to translate woodworking skill into a product for the bicycle boom. The Old Hickory, as its best-known model was called, was promoted for vibration absorption as well. Here again, the argument was thin, and even the maker probably had doubts. Thus, Tonk was careful to detail its machine with the most elegant metal work ever applied to a production bicycle. If wealthier wheelmen sought a machine that set them apart from the crowd, the Old Hickory filled the bill until around 1900, when the company gave up bicycle making and went back to its true occupation which was furniture manufacturing.

Enormous sales were enjoyed by bicycle manufacturers in the 1890s, peaking in 1897

tunity to study the subject in the bicycle press. A "56 gear," for example, meant "that one revolution of the cranks will turn the driving wheel [whatever diameter it may be] an amount equal to the circumference of a 56-inch wheel," as the *Bulletin* explained. "It is common for racing men to ride machines geared to seventy or more, while it would be an exceptionally long rider who could reach a 60-inch wheel of the old [high-wheel] style." This suggested the valid conclusion that the safety bicycle was an improvement over the high-wheeler (or "ordinary," as the old models were now called, in contradistinction to the more sophisticated safety bicycles). Additional theories published on the subject of gearing ranged from the obvious to impenetrable.

The bicycle boom created interest in all manner of applications of the technology. They included cycles with blades for the ice pond, and ambulances to transport the sick and wounded. One of the more reasonable ideas floated at the time was the water cycle which was reported to travel a quarter of a mile upstream in four and a half minutes. It did not displace the standard oar however, and was never more than a curiosity.

when some 3,000 firms were doing business in America making cycles, cycle parts, and "sundries." Estimates are that more than two million bicycles were sold in that year. Of course, a saturation point was inevitable, and the industry did everything it could to postpone it. One of its most pervasive efforts to prolong the bicycle boom was the practice of planned obsolescence. While some improvements in steel tubing and suspension designs were real advances in technology, many redesigns were not. Manufacturers might move the front sprocket back or forth to suggest improved torque, for example, whether such a claim was justified or not. At cycle shows, new colors were introduced with more than a modicum of fanfare. One maker from California even claimed that when his bicycle changed its color to blue, it won more professional races than any other cycle. And these false claims represented but the tip of the iceberg.

Another aspect of cycling with which many people became excessively preoccupied was the science of gearing. Enthusiasts began throwing gear numbers around in the most casual conversation, and they took every oppor-

During the bicycle boom the industry took to printing lavish catalogues. Some of these publications were masculine, even imperial, such as that of Monarch in 1900, but most of them suggested that women had a role in the bicycle boom as well as men. The notion of courtship on a bicycle was hardly concealed in the Pope Manufacturing Company's William Morris-like catalogue for 1896.

The Wright Van Cleve (here in reproduction) was a partly successful predecessor to the wind-tunnel needed to develop data for the optimal design of wings on flying planes after their famous first flight at Kitty Hawk in 1903. The Wrights reamined in the bicycle business until 1904, at which point they gave their full attention to airplanes, where they apparently reasoned the compeition was less intense.

Some bicycle makers did take the art of bicycle making into loftier realms of science, however. A pair of them, perhaps the most famous bicycle makers ever, lived in Dayton, Ohio. In the beginning of their career, Orville and Wilbur Wright seemed not unlike thousands of other mechanics and manufacturers in the trade during the boom years. They established a prosperous and competent bicycle concern but would have been all but forgotten if they had not applied themselves to a more eccentric category of engineering.

In everything they did, the Wrights possessed seemingly disproportionate curiosity for the latest technologies. As young men they were first intrigued by the printing business, which tested their mechanical skills. In the early 1890s, they fixed on the bicycle. In fact, the younger Orville was quite a scorcher at this time and won several local races. In the early stages of the bicycle boom in Dayton, the brothers quickly demonstrated a talent for adjusting and repairing bicycles and, ultimately, for building them. They opened their first shop in 1892 and worked hard to make a living, al-

though they took enough time out the following year to visit Chicago and the World's Columbian Exposition. Bicycles and aeronautics both were featured at this world's fair, and both areas commanded the Wright brothers' attention.

As young businessmen, the Wrights developed a reputation for honesty, which in the bicycle trade meant that they were always reluctant to carry the sundries of doubtful use being pushed at that time. These included mud guards, which their makers claimed scraped tires clean but which often got tangled in the spokes. More extravagant distractions in the bicycle industry at this time were things like water bicycles and ice bicycles. The serious-minded Wrights wanted no part of such items. They were interested, at least at first, only in what made a better bicycle.

In their fifteen years in the business, the Wrights moved to progressively larger quarters five times. While the business carried various makes and models, the brothers worked hardest at building and designing a bicycle of their own: the Van Cleve, which was named after a

relative. This was a 22-pound, top-of-the-line, machine. It was a good value at $65 in 1896 when it went into production. The frame was brazed, the hubs were of the Wrights' own design, and many of the components came from the best makers of the era. Building such a bicycle was time-consuming work, and it is believed that the brothers never built more than 150—and this number included the cheaper St. Clair, which used a stock frame purchased from the Pope factory.

The Wrights made little money in bicycles—several thousand dollars a year in these boom times. The reason they didn't earn more probably was that their minds were wandering elsewhere. One could have assumed that the restless and mechanical Wrights might have taken up a new interest in another invention on the horizon: the automobile. Instead of cars, though, Orville and Wilbur showed an interest in something truly fantastic for the mid-1890s, namely aviation. Other mechanical people were talking about powered flight at the time, and *Scientific American,* while faithfully covering the bicycle industry in every issue, also reported from time to time on the adventures of a German inventor, Otto Lilienthal. Lilienthal's experimental gliders were the direct predecessors to flying machines. They provided ample inspiration for people like the Wright Brothers, who were quickly obsessed with the idea of building a powered flyer.

It had already been predicted that the inventors who would defy gravity might well come from the ranks of bicycle makers. This was because many qualities necessary to cycle making appeared to be essential in flight as well. Lightness of structural materials was an obvious one. An imperturbable sense of balance and equilibrium was another. Beyond that was something that can only be called freedom. "It is not uncommon for the cyclist in the first flash of enthusiasm which quickly follows the unpleasantness of taming the steel steed, to remark: 'Wheeling is just like flying!'" wrote the *Aeronautical Annual,* which covered experiments in heavier-than-air flight even prior to the Wrights.

In the Wright Brothers' case, bicycle technology proved indispensable to aeronautics. In their first successful flying machine, wings were stabilized with spoke wire. Propeller shafts were

1898 Rex Cycle
Rex Cycle Co., Chicago, Illinois
Late in the bicycle boom, the Rex Cycle was an attempt to cushion the ride without the use of springs or shock absorbers, which some considered unsafe and uncomfortable. With its long "backbone" and third wheel, the Rex was promoted as having all the advantages of a rigid frame in addition to a smoother ride. It was "superior to the bicycle in comfort, safety, speed, light-running, and durability," its catalogue declared. Sadly, the bicycle boom was almost over, and the Rex never got the chance in the marketplace that some thought it deserved.

IMPROVED DROP FRAME.

Made of imported seamless steel tubing and steel drop forgings.
For style, durability and elasticity it has no equal.

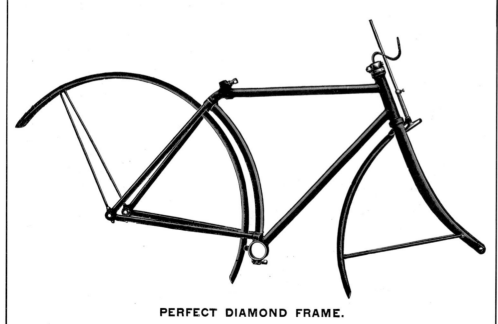

PERFECT DIAMOND FRAME.

Made of imported seamless steel tubing and steel drop forgings.
Proven to be the lightest and strongest.

made of steel tubing. And since too-great torsion was a risk to their airplane's lightweight frame, the Wrights used two propellers at lower speed, instead of one running high. Transmission was by trusty chain drives.

The Wrights bicycle background also came in handy in less predictable ways. After their first famous flight at Kitty Hawk in 1903, the restless brothers were certain that they could improve on their invention, specifically by achieving the optimal size and shape of the wings, if they could determine the theoretical coefficient of air pressure on curved surfaces. Determined to find this formula through live tests, they discovered that primitive wind tunnels proved insufficient to the task. A partially successful solution to this problem came when they affixed wind vanes on the handlebars of a bicycle and rode like mad to generate sufficient draft to obtain their desired results.

Flying machines were still only a dream when another revolution was ushered in, or accompanied by, the bicycle boom. The women's rights movement surged in the 1890s, which was also the decade in which women took to the wheel. Bicycles meant many things to the women who rode them, especially freedom from virtual imprisonment in the home. To its credit, the L.A.W. wholeheartedly supported the right of women to ride bicycles. But there were limits, as voiced by a writer in the *Bulletin* in 1896: "Immense discredit is brought upon cycling by women who are rough, masculine, and noisy in their habits and tones of thought . . . Why, because they cycle, should they talk and laugh at the top of their voices, affect rough ways, and try to copy men in all their most undesirable points?" In fact, the industry had recently devised the dropped frame so women could mount and dismount without indecorous display. It was thus possible to preserve femininity as a wheelwoman, though another writer opined that "there is one class of woman who brings discredit upon her pastime, while all the time she thinks she is doing it a world of good. This is the woman who talks of cycles, and nothing else." Lady "scorchers" who rode fast and terrified all others on the road were also considered a blight.

Although it was often shocking in the Gay 90s, the appearance of women on bicycles was not sudden. Women first appeared on bicycles

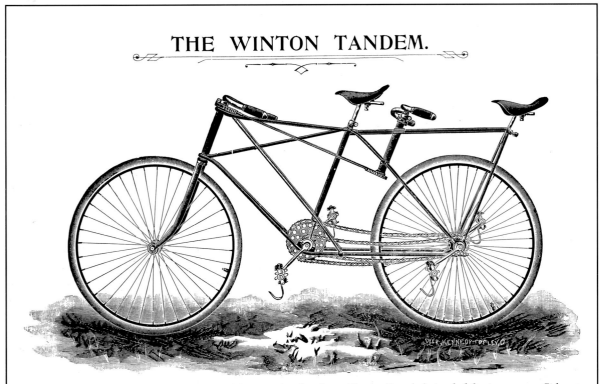

THE WINTON TANDEM.

THE WINTON TANDEM, as will be seen by the above illustration, is intended for two men. It has a very strongly braced frame, built on the same lines as our models A and B. The steering device is something new and very effective, doing away with the usual rod connecting the ends of both handle bars, and instead has a chain running on a small sprocket on each handle bar post, connected by two straight steel rods; special chain gearing; wheels, 30 in.; 1¾ in. front and 2 in. rear tires; gear, 72. We have in course of construction a tandem suitable for a lady and gentleman, which will be ready for delivery about April 1st.

Weight, 48 Lbs.   Price, $225.00.

— 14 —

OPPOSITE PAGE: Simple and elegant, the basic diamond frame became the standard design during the bicycle boom. With good steel tubing, it lent itself to modification for women, a development which came more naturally in America than it did in the early years in Europe. In this 1892 catalogue, the Western Wheel Works of Chicago showed how its standard model was cleanly adapted with a "dropped frame" for use by wheelwomen who might continue to wear flowing dresses and not necessarily controversial bloomers.

LEFT TOP: In 1897, the police department of New York City conducted enough tests to adopt the bicycle—specifically the Wolff-American—for a number of purposes, including catching and arresting "scorchers," or recklessly rapid bicyclists, on the roadways of the city. That same year the New York Department of Street Cleaning also purchased a fleet of Wolff-Americans which gave "entire satisfaction," according to an endorsement provided by City Hall.

LEFT BOTTOM: The knotty problem of steering the tandem led to a variety of solutions. While the chivalrous gentleman should naturally escort his lady from the rear seat of a bicycle built for two, it remained essential that he should maintain complete control of the vehicle. The addition of rods connecting the rear handlebars to the steering mechanism was introduced and adopted by many tandem makers, and advertised here in 1893.

accompanied by male escorts on tandems, which had been imported from England at least by 1883. These earliest tandems were side-by-side models on three or four wheels, many of which were designed and marketed by James Starley, of Coventry. It is assumed that Starley was motivated by the feeling that bicycles "engendered an unsociable feeling among the priv-

ileged few," as noted by a contemporary scribe. Starley's tandem developed first as a "lever-driven quadricycle" which he introduced in 1877. He soon converted to chain-drive with cranks and pedals for both riders.

The importance of one aspect of Starley's invention of the sociable bicycle transcends even his inadvertent role in female emancipation. It was the differential, then (and now) essential for any powered vehicle with two wheels on a rear axle. After many presumed mishaps in experiments with sociable tricycles and quadricycles, due to unequal force on the two driving wheels when turning, Starley joined the two sides of the rear axle with a "balancing gear." The system maintained equal force on both wheels in straightaways and varied force on turns. The inside wheel thus rolled more slowly than the outside and maintained precious equilibrium as a result.

Invented at approximately the same time was the two-wheeled tandem, reportedly developed by English inventors Albone and Wilson. In their most advanced design, the woman took the front position, with the man behind, as chivalry of the period demanded. While the man's rear cranks properly applied most of the driving force, the question of who should steer was a more ticklish problem. Albone and Wilson resolved it to their satisfaction by connecting handlebars fore and aft with steel rods, thus giving the man some control over steering. The coupled-handlebar concept was hardly ideal, for obvious reasons, and was later abandoned—forcing men and women to make certain compromises related to decorum and ultimate control.

Nevertheless, tandems became vehicles of undeniable romance. "More happy unions were cemented on tandem bicycles because romantic lovers developed a rhythmic sense and thus became attached to each other," wrote one magazine at the time. They facilitated elopements as well. In the aptly named town of Narrowsburg, New York, a young maid rode off from her parents' home on the family tandem with her lover and got married. The story was particularly dismal for the father because his wife had counseled against ever getting into bicycles at all, as she was certain that they were a corrupter of morals.

Of course, the tandem was only a stopgap measure as far as women and bicycles were concerned. Women quickly determined that there was something preferable in riding independently. One wheelwoman writing in the *L.A.W. Bulletin* during the bicycle boom put it succinctly: "It may be said that there is no matrimonial trap more effective than a 'bicycle built for two,' or even two bicycles built for one apiece, if the conditions are all favorable,—

moonlight night, lonely road, etc." But a New Woman, as the writer implied she was, could do quite well on a bicycle by herself, thank you. A bicycle "never talks back, and responds quickly and easily to the slightest wish. It never growls (only squeaks a little) when its meals are not ready, or its buttons off. Does not swear, smoke, chew or drink. Again, its whereabouts can always be depended upon."

A truly revolutionary change attributable to the bicycle at this time was wrought in the form of female dress. The wearing of bloomers by women became widespread. Corsets were largely discarded (though "bicycle corsets" were available), and many women dedicated themselves to "rational dress." For most wheelwomen, the change was only practical. Writer Maria E. Ward, author of *Bicycling For Ladies*, advised evenly: "Clothing should be most carefully selected, with the view of an equal distribution of weight and even thickness of material; it should have no constricting, no tight bands

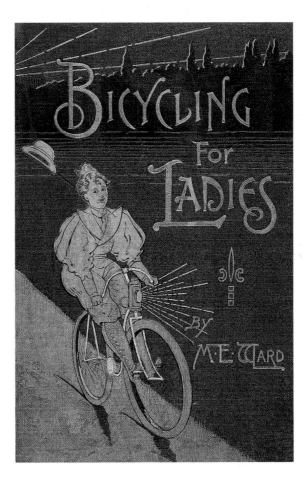

By the time Maria Ward published *Bicycling For Ladies* (subtitled "The Common Sense of Bicycling"), the writer could all but discount those who did not understand the appropriateness of females *en biciclette*. "The cyclists, to the stationary observer or the comparatively stationary pedestrian, is such a fleeting instantaneosity that, unless thrown among enthusiasts over the sport, few of the unenlightened would be tempted to try it."

1897 Tally-Ho Tandem
Maumee Cycle Co., Toledo, Ohio
The tandem conundrum—that the gentleman should ride behind his fair maiden—led to a number of adjustments, such as a 30-inch wheel on the rear and a "donkey-back" for sight lines over the coiffeur of his lady. The real problem, of course, was the steering. Like many other tandems, the Tally-Ho addressed it with steel rods from the a shaft connecting the rear handlebars to the front fork. The device was marginally successful, though it did represent the first clear battle of wills between many a courting couple.

By 1897, bloomers were a common sight, as were women on bicycles. Less common were ladies lining up for races, though Tillie Anderson, pictured here with medals pinned to her lapels, was the country's most famous female champion when this picture was made around 1897.

anywhere, but should permit absolute freedom of movement."

Rational dress influenced all society, not just wheelwomen, but the predictable reaction against these trends tended to focus on bicycle people. A writer for the *New York Times* editorialized in 1896 that the girl in bloomers "was not the wildly beautiful creature many of the writers, especially the bicycle enthusiasts, would have one believe . . . She does not stand the glare of sunshine well."

Yet bloomers, along with the bicycle, overcame all conservatives. In Chicago, for example, a matron cycled peaceably in a new bloomer outfit through Lincoln Park unmolested until one Emmanuel Engstrom could not, or did not, resist the temptation to "hoot" at the lady. The police promptly arrested the man, who claimed in court that he did not hoot— rather, he "chortled," an act which the defendant claimed was beyond his reasonable control. The judge rejected the argument and assessed a moderate fine upon this boorish male.

Also in Chicago, a dance given in a Jackson Park hall was billed for bicyclists, admission limited to people in the appropriate garb. It was a great success, with 400 attendees, at least half of them women in bloomers. Also on hand were some 5,000 spectators who came to witness the odd, even risqué, spectacle. And a reporter from the *Chicago Record* was there as well, giving the event slightly more publicity than it was ready for. "'Bloomers beat dresses all to pieces,'" one male cyclist was quoted. "'They don't interfere with the fun, you can't step on them nor tear them, and you don't have to get a carriage to take the girl home. Bloomers are all right.'" But not to everyone. The following week, when cyclists attempted a second bloomer dance, the gathering was broken up by police who threatened to arrest the lot of them for undignified public behavior.

It must be pointed out that not all cyclists were libertines. Bicycles appealed to sterner sorts as well, such as the worthy souls of the Women's Christian Temperance Union (W.C.T.U.). To early warnings that cycling could lead to drink, the L.A.W. was quick to argue that this was not at all the case. Collisions and falls were hazards even for stone-sober wheelman, and getting sloshed really was out of the question, the organization claimed. Then came

1897 Ladies' New Star
New Star Co., Smithville, New Jersey
The New Star Co. was the successor company to H.B. Smith Machine. Both firms were active innovators. In this case, designers reckoned that levers attached to leather belts and rotating drums on the rear wheel would prompt women to turn away from cumbersome cranks and dirty chains. It was a bright idea that never caught on. This 28-inch model is a rare collector's item today.

Frances Willard, president of the W.C.T.U. She not only bought a bicycle and learned to ride, she even wrote a book on the subject. *How I Learned to Ride a Bicycle: With Some Reflections Along the Way* was an earnest treatise on the pleasures and virtues of the road, "with pleasant little half-concealed sermonettes," according to a reviewer for the *L.A.W. Bulletin.* The bicycle fraternity probably did appreciate Miss Willard's endorsement, but her book strained their patience a little. "Just how she managed to think these noble and perfectly proper thoughts while trying to learn to ride a wheel will puzzle a good many beginners," the reviewer went on. Moralizing on the subject of temperance did not help mounting and dismounting in the least, he argued, and furthermore, many wheelmen might well enjoy a malted beverage, despite Miss Willard's objections, after a hard day of riding.

Even independent women were vulnerable, however, to the growing class of charlatans and profiteers who invented needs and products particular to bicyclists of the fairer sex. Those who diagnosed a female problem associated with cycling, ponderously termed "heating of the blood," were no doubt honest physicians. But the remedies for the malady that ensued were of doubtful sincerity indeed. One patent medicine concocted and advertised for the purpose was Payne's Celery Tonic, which was certain only to separate the wheelwoman from her money.

Fortunately, the bicycling community was mostly conscientious about health and wise to quackery. In another issue of the *L.A.W. Bulletin*, in 1896, a physician and cyclist named Dr. J. D. Albright of Akron, Pennsylvania, warned strenuously against taking "aromatic sulfuric acid," advertised as a way to check perspiration. "Perspiration is not the only secretion that is checked when this drug is taken," he wrote. He equated the use of these pills to "plugging the muzzle of a musket then pulling the trigger." It was a particular threat to women, he noted, who were naturally adverse to working up a good sweat. Fortunately, sulfuric acid was one bicycle sundry that never took hold. But this was a rare triumph for reason as the bicycle boom reached high pitch.

LEFT: 1898 Chilion Ladies' Model M. D. Stebbins Manufacturing Co., Springfield, Massachusetts
The Chilion's makers made many claims for the wooden bicycle. The natural qualities of the wood included resistance to buckling when a rider hit a curb with force that would certainly compromise a steel frame. This did not eliminate the possibility of splintering after too many such encounters with rocks and hard places. One thing that could be said with certainty, however, was that Chilions did not rust. Nor did the aluminum-bronze lugs.

ABOVE: In 1894, Wheel Around the Hub was an annual event for Boston-area clubs to join together for a two-day circumnavigation of the city's periphery, though it was never too serious to prevent participants from stopping for a malted beverage along the way. Here, they gather at Cobb's Tavern in Canton, Massuchussetts.

Chapter Four

Bicycle Racers: America's Early Sports Heroes

BICYCLE RACING WAS a natural accompaniment to the bicycle boom, but there was always a question about its moral purpose. It was quickly popular, even madly so, and greatly lucrative, a fact which caused no small concern among the leadership of the League of American Wheelmen. The L.A.W. regarded itself as the guardian of cycling and claimed without irony that its work—on behalf of amateur cycling and good roads everywhere—benefited democracy, commerce, health, and even "brute creation" (since the league objective of better roads improved the lives of draft animals).

Thus, it was a matter of some embarrassment to the bishops of bicycledom that one of the most popular entertainment spectacles of the 1890s was a kind of endurance contest on bicycles called "six-day racing." Six-days took place on oval tracks, with a pack of cyclists racing day and night with minimal rest. As the days wore on, these events grew ghastly. Exhausted to the point of numbness, riders frequently collided. But promoters pressed them on. Spectators came and went over the duration of the race. Gamblers of every stripe took wagers. The public loved it and so did the newspapers. "Whirling demons who ride between walls of shrieking faces" was how the *New York Times* described the early six-days. Riders normally had to ride more than 1,200 miles to qualify for any prize money at all.

RIGHT: 1910 Racycle Roadster
Miami Cycle & Manufacturing Co., Middletown, Ohio
The boom was over, but racing was still popular. Thus bicycle makers did everything they could to imply that their roadsters were very nearly raceworthy. The Racycle had the lines and look of a track bicycle. Curiously, its crank bearings were outside the chain sprocket, perhaps a design feature from race mechanics. Also, the sprockets were larger than normal and may have looked very fast—though seventy teeth in front and twenty-two in the rear resulted in the same gearing as most recreational road bicycles of the day.

The famous racers of the high-wheel bicycle era did not adapt instantly to the safety, but when they did, the sport became a national sensation. *Bearings* magazine produced several portraits of the top competitors on the circuit in 1893. Eddie "Cannon" Bald and others were well-known stars by then. While racing authorities attempted to maintain the amateur status of the American sport, racers always competed for prizes and routinely converted their booty to cash. By the mid-1890s, professional racing was accepted, and noble amateurs quickly became wealthy and celebrated sports stars.

BOWLER.
VAN NORMAN,
PHOTO.
SPRINGFIELD.

The "single six," which meant a single rider pedaling as many as twenty hours a day, was finally outlawed, but not before Charlie Miller, a German immigrant living in Chicago, won something like national celebrity for his iron-man feats on this circuit. Showmanship, of course, was as important as athletic prowess. One of the most famous six-day races ever staged was in New York in 1898, when an altar was set in the midfield of the track and Miller, "King of the Single Sixes," was married during one of his breaks from riding. (He was wearing pink and white tights for the occasion.) Reports of the event were embellished with side stories that other riders in the race were having hallucinations while they continued to race. One believed his own sweetheart was being swept away by another man in the stands; another claimed that he was being poisoned. Miller nat-

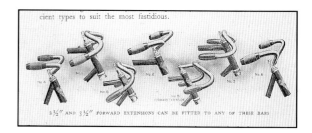

cient types to suit the most fastidious.

2½" AND 3½" FORWARD EXTENSIONS CAN BE FITTED TO ANY OF THESE BARS

urally won this race, as did those who bet on him.

The idea of garnering sensational press was via athletic feats never far from the surface of the bicycle industry—the L.A.W. notwithstanding. Publicity-seeking went back to the high-wheeler days of the 1880s, when the Col. Pope-supported *Outing* magazine sent Englishman Thomas Stevens on a bicycle trip around the world and published installments of his adventures as he dispatched them along the way. His "terrestrial circumcycloration," as one reporter called the trip, was inspired by Jules Verne's *Around the World in Eighty Days* as much as by the growing enthusiasm for cycling.

Stevens became, in the two years and eight months of this trip, one of the world's most famous men. As he started out in San Francisco, he was given a magnificent send-off, escorted by local cycling clubs that lionized any man daring enough to undertake such an adventure. In small towns, he was chased by children. In

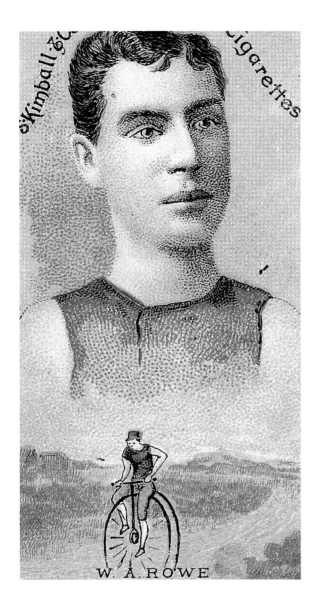

W. A. ROWE

Wesson (perhaps similar to those advertised in the cycling magazines for serious wheelmen), and his way was cleared. Never was Stevens thwarted from his purpose.

That was, until he returned to America.

Completing his circuit, he got off the boat in San Francisco to a tumultuous reception. As he crossed the country again, this time by train, he was entertained by bicycle clubs in every city he visited. But then something strange happened. En route, it occurred to him that his membership in the League of American Wheelmen had lapsed while he was abroad. He quickly shot off a letter to Boston to have his card renewed, mentioning in this note that nothing impressed foreign dignitaries quite like the wheel-and-wings badge worn by L.A.W. members.

A week later, he had his reply. "The King of the Cycling World," as he was called, was denied renewed membership. The reason given was a race that he had ridden in Boston some two years before as he passed through on his famous trip. Stevens was at that time new to the L.A.W. and unacquainted with its rules. He innocently competed in a twenty-four-hour race, for which he was promised a portion of the gate receipts. He never did get paid, but he shrugged and blithely left Boston to continue his global journey. Yet because of this brush with professionalism, Stevens was banned from the esteemed society of cyclists.

The Lure of Professionalism

Professionalism was an issue that would continue to beset the L.A.W. for the next decade. It never truly came to grips with the fact that the noble amateurism of cycling was often overshadowed by its wide popularity, which meant that "the wheel" was not just a source of spiritual uplift in the world of cycling but one of great revenue as well. Initially, the taint of professionalism in league-sanctioned racing was obscure enough to be ignored. The high-wheel racers were generally well-heeled chaps, traveling from track to track, pedaling for the pure joy of it, perhaps getting prizes or a little money well under the table.

Among the first stars of the sport was George M. Hendee, a graceful and handsome young man who became well known in the 1880s in the polite society of cyclists. When an

OPPOSITE PAGE LEFT: Paddy Bowler, later a corrupt and corpulent alderman among many such individuals in the Chicago City Council, first won fame as a sprinter and six-day racer around the turn of the century.

OPPOSITE PAGE RIGHT: Racing technology provided countless options for everyday riders as suggested by the selection of handlebars in this 1902 catalogue.

LEFT: In the 1880s, cigarettes were sold with small cards picturing the great sports stars of the age. Among them was W.A. Rowe, amateur champion in the employ of the Colonel Albert Pope's firm which made Columbia high-wheelers.

the West, amongst curious Indians and hard-drinking cowboys, adventures were many. Later, in Europe, his fame had spread to such an extent that he received proposals of marriage from strange and beautiful women who intercepted him along the way.

Perhaps the most exciting episodes of the Stevens saga took place in the wilds of Asia, expanses that were ruled—at least in the American imagination—by brigands and murderers. Bravely he pedaled on. In Kurdistan, he was assailed by vicious-looking sheep dogs. Later, in the highlands of the Caucasus Mountains, he was accosted by sword-waving villains. In each case, he needed only to show his Smith and

George M. Hendee won the first national cycling championship in Boston in 1882 on a high-wheeler, and went on to accumulate many medals and much honor. An amateur athlete, he later made money from cycling by manufacturing a bicycle, the Indian, which was outfitted with a motor in 1901. The Indian motorcycle, made by the Hendee Manufacturing Company of Springfield, Massachusetts, was America's first production model, and it made Hendee and partner Oscar Hedstrom wealthy ex-amateur racers.

GEO. M. HENDEE.
AMATEUR CHAMPION BICYCLIST OF THE UNITED STATES.

RIGHT TOP AND BOTTOM: A. A. Zimmerman, considered America's first international athletic star, made the transition from high-wheelers to safety bicycles which he raced in America and Europe until around the turn of the century. Though he wrote a book on fitness and cycling, there were also reports that he could smoke and tipple most of the night with friends and still win his race the next day with room to spare.

upstart by the name of W. A. Rowe defeated him soundly in an 1887 race in Springfield, Massachusetts, it was said that the entire grandstands wept to see the mantle of a champion passed on so abruptly. The skill and courage of these riders obscured the fact that Hendee was supplied with Victor cycles and was getting money from Overman, and that Roe was astride a Columbia and on the payroll of Pope.

By the 1890s, however, a new crop of riders had come into the limelight on the new, more accessible safety bicycle. As the "safety" broadened ridership of the bicycle, it also changed the nature of racing. It was a larger pastime, more enthusiastic, and more money was naturally at stake. It also made room in bicycling for more broadly popular heroes, such as Miller in the single sixes, and such as a young man from New Jersey, Arthur A. Zimmerman. It was Zimmerman who changed "amateur" bicycle racing from a sport for the wealthy to something that had almost universal appeal.

"Zimmy" first made a name for himself in the 1880s, at races on a circuit that included many horse tracks at state and county fairs. He made the transition from high-wheeler to safety bicycle around 1891. He made this change reluctantly, but when he did, Zimmerman became an ever-present advertisement for the new chain-drive machines with pneumatic tires (which he also preferred). Zimmy had fantastic leg speed and could pedal so fast that he kept his bicycle at a lower gear than most competitors did. He became famous for short bursts of speed, and the classic Zimmerman strategy consisted of holding back until the last lap, when he surged forward and crossed the tape comfortably ahead of the rest of the field.

As Zimmerman entered his prime he was still an amateur. For winning his races, he was awarded prizes, not money. Common prizes on the racing circuit in this time included diamond stick pins, which racers normally sold to local jewelers for cash. As the popularity of cycle racing increased, so did prizes of this sort—pianos, parcels of land, and deeds to houses were among the commodities that Zimmerman hauled in for his efforts. This practice soon rankled the protectors of amateurism in the L.A.W.; where Zimmerman was keeping all of his prizes was a matter of great speculation. The ill-kept secret was, of course, that he was selling them. In 1892, for example, when he captured the mile sprint at the nation's premier meet at Springfield, Zimmy got a pair of horses, a harness, and a buckboard for his efforts. The star blithely accepted the prizes, and in all likelihood sold them for what they were worth, about $1,000.

Later in 1892, Zimmerman was invited to England which had what was considered the most distinguished, and purely amateur, racing circuit in the world. Zimmy's success in England secured him a place as one of America's first international sports stars, winning the English national championships at the 1-, 5-, and 25-mile distances. Then, in the 50-mile race, Zimmerman's fame reached its peak. He was up against a field that included English distance star Frank Shorland. In Zimmy's characteristic way he held back until most of the competition had fallen back from the pack. After more than two hours, only Zimmerman and Shorland were left, and with the finish line in sight, Zimmerman alone had the strength left in his legs to sprint ahead and win by several lengths.

The American's triumph impressed England, especially the English bicycle maker Raleigh, which the following year supplied him with bicycles and probably made handsome, if

clandestine, payments. Zimmy showed up in Raleigh advertising. He also came out with a book, *Points For Cyclists With Training,* that was underwritten by Raleigh. The presumption of Zimmerman's amateurism was waning, and the following year, when he returned to England for another season, he was banned. The fans loved him, but English cycling officials made a long list of his violations and sent him away. In response, Zimmerman simply sailed across the Channel to France, where professional racing was standard, and where Zimmy did very well at the famous Paris velodrome, the Buffalo (so called because it had been the site of Buffalo Bill's Wild West Show some years before). Win-

One of the top velodromes in the nation was in Newark, New Jersey, where cycling established itself as one of the most important professional sports of the first quarter of the century. Greats like Alf Goullet (leading), Frank Kramer—shown here in one of many match races that attracted major crowds in the 1920s—considered it their home track. Also in the neighborhood was the bicycle shop of Pop Brennan, one of the greatest racing mechanics of the period. (Brennan's shop survived into the 1990s, though it has long since moved from Newark proper.)

CATALOGUE No. 9

The Tribune Blue Streak was a favorite of racers. It weighed about 20 pounds with 28-inch wheels, and tooled steel bearings. Many top racers chose the bicycle, though they were encouraged by heavy sponsorships. The Blue Streak achieved immortality in 1899 when Charlie "Mile-a-Minute" Murphy rode in the draft of a speeding train on Long Island and shattered all previous records by going just better than 60 miles per hour.

membership in the League of American Wheelmen had lapsed while he was abroad. He quickly shot off a letter to Boston to have his card renewed, mentioning in this note that nothing impressed foreign dignitaries quite like the wheel-and-wings badge worn by L.A.W. members.

A week later, he had his reply. "The King of the Cycling World," as he was called, was denied renewed membership. The reason given was a race that he had ridden in Boston some two years before as he passed through on his famous trip. Stevens was at that time new to the L.A.W. and unacquainted with its rules. He innocently competed in a twenty-four-hour race, for which he was promised a portion of the gate receipts. He never did get paid, but he shrugged and blithely left Boston to continue his global journey. Yet because of this brush with professionalism, Stevens was banned from the esteemed society of cyclists.

The Lure of Professionalism

Professionalism was an issue that would continue to beset the L.A.W. for the next decade. It never truly came to grips with the fact that the noble amateurism of cycling was often overshadowed by its wide popularity, which meant that "the wheel" was not just a source of spiritual uplift in the world of cycling but one of great revenue as well. Initially, the taint of professionalism in league-sanctioned racing was obscure enough to be ignored. The high-wheel racers were generally well-heeled chaps, traveling from track to track, pedaling for the pure joy of it, perhaps getting prizes or a little money well under the table.

Among the first stars of the sport was George M. Hendee, a graceful and handsome young man who became well known in the 1880s in the polite society of cyclists. When an upstart by the name of W. A. Rowe defeated him soundly in an 1887 race in Springfield, Massachusetts, it was said that the entire grandstands wept to see the mantle of a champion passed on so abruptly. The skill and courage of these riders obscured the fact that Hendee was supplied with Victor cycles and was getting money from Overman, and that Roe was astride a Columbia and on the payroll of Pope.

By the 1890s, however, a new crop of riders had come into the limelight on the new,

"Dayton Racer"

MODEL 123

PRICE $50.00

TRUE AS STEEL AND SKILL CAN MAKE THEM

DAYTON BICYCLES

1913

THE·DAVIS·SEWING·MACHINE·CO.

MAKERS

DAYTON, OHIO.

The Dayton Racer, made by the Davis Sewing Machine Company in Dayton, Ohio, was a top machine for amateur racers. By 1913, the model pictured here included a number of racing features, such as adjustable handlebars and a shorter wheelbase, which improved maneuverability and acceleration.

Still, most Americans were fascinated by Zimmerman, whose victories seemed effortless. In 1895, for example, a *Harper's Weekly* writer covering a big race described Zimmerman's pre-race demeanor in which "all rules of training were held by him in abeyance for a week. Mr. Zimmerman was chatty—he was convivial. He daily and nightly joined with zest in every boyish prank and sport until tired nature bade his companions seek their rest. In the small hours of the morning when they did so Mr. Zimmerman kept the pace by taking to the verandah and smoking cigars with whoever was enticed by his agreeable companionship." Then, with three hours sleep, Zimmerman went out and broke a time record—in this case completing a mile in 1 minute and 57-4/5 seconds.

The Orient "Oriten" never distinguished itself as a pace vehicle for racers, but it did demonstrate that the Waltham Manufacturing Company had mastered the art of multicycle building. It weighed more than 300 pounds, was 23 feet in length, and reached a top speed, according to records, of 45 miles per hour. The front rider required substantial strength for steering. Braking was achieved by back pedaling, the force of which was the primary responsibility of the tenth rider.

Zimmerman quit top-line competition in 1897 and retired to New Jersey, where he purchased a hotel in which he happily greeted many admirers. He also put his name on a new bicycle making concern. The Zimmerman Manufacturing Company, in Freehold, New Jersey, put out a line of high-quality bicycles that would capture, it was hoped, a portion of the market on the strength of Zimmerman's reputation and without expensive paid advertising. "Zimmys," as the bicycles were called, did make their mark, but even the Flying Yankee soon found that fame was fleeting and advertising essential. Meanwhile, the professional race circuit continued to grow, and sponsors of active racers were making more noise than ever before.

The Major Taylor Saga

Many more names became famous toward the end of the 1890s and through the next decade, as America went increasingly mad for bicycle racing. Many skilled racers of this period represented frequently ambitious manufacturers with plenty of money to promote their supposedly new and better bicycles. Perhaps the most fascinating and enduring story of professional cycling in this period was that of Marshall Taylor, an African-American who became one of America's first world champion athletes. Though he came to a sad end and his name no longer rings with the clarity of Joe Louis or Jackie Robinson, "Major" Taylor, as he became known, did as much as either of the other two to focus the nation's attention on racial prejudice in the United States. His accomplishments came in a period when Jim Crow laws were vicious and enforced in some parts of the country by lynchings.

Even as a child, Taylor possessed some qualities that enabled him to rise above the normal indignities of racial prejudice. Growing up in Indianapolis, he was befriended by the child of a family for whom Taylor's father was stable keeper. As the two boys, one black and one white, grew inseparable, the wealthy employer brought young Marshall to live in his home. There were two important outcomes from this uncommon arrangement. One was that the young black boy developed manner and confidence that enabled him to operate in the white-dominated world. The other was that he was given a bicycle—a very expensive toy for a child at the time—which he learned to ride with uncommon skill.

A measure of fame came at an early age. In 1892, when he was about thirteen years old, Marshall took his bike to the shop of the Hay & Willits Manufacturing Company in Indianapolis for some repairs. When the work was completed, Marshall took some pleasure in showing the men in the establishment some of the "fancy mounts" that he had perfected. Mr. Hay, in particular, was impressed and asked to see more, and before the afternoon was through he had the youngster doing tricks out on the street, where a crowd quickly gathered. Hay & Willits was a growing concern—it would later gain notoriety for its "automatic hub brake," an early

coaster brake—and was naturally anxious to draw any kind of public attention to itself. So young Marshall was hired, outfitted in a military suit with brass buttons, and given the name "Major." Other duties involved sweeping and cleaning the shop, but at 4:00 PM each day he was out on the sidewalk, giving a performance and attracting spectators.

It was almost against his will that Major Taylor first became a racer. Later that year, he went out to watch the start of a local 10-mile handicapped road race. While he had dreamt that he might someday race, he had no intention of getting involved this day, particularly since most of the riders were a good ten years older than he. Then, just before the starting gun, Mr. Hay fairly dragged Taylor to the starting line. The boy was terrified and began to cry, but he started the race with a small handicap, and in the end came away with a medal. It was the beginning of a brilliant racing career, as well as the beginning of much vile prejudice in

Race managers trained their athletes, found sponsors to pay expenses, scheduled races, and didn't let go at the starting line until they had given their man the strongest push they could muster. Pictured is the start of a sprint at the Newark Velodrome. Frank Kramer, second from left, was world sprint champion in 1912, a title he won on this very track.

1910 Truss-Bridge
Roadster Iver Johnson,
Fitchburg, Massachusetts
Iver Johnson's notoriety grew as the
sponsor of Major Taylor when the
racer's career was peaking in
Europe. So the company produced
a bicycle with many features of
Taylor's track model, such as light
steel tubing and racing handlebars
specified by Taylor himself. In the
interest of durability, designers
added the truss beneath the cross
bar for the everyday rider, who was
more likely than Major to beat his
bicycle along bad roads.

Major Taylor climbed near the top of American cycle racing in the 1890s, then went abroad where racism in the popular sport was far less harsh than in his own country. Here, Taylor starts a race at the Friedenau track in Berlin in 1901. This was the first of fifty-seven races on a tour of seventeen European cities. Of those races he won forty-two, and his worldwide fame grew despite the fact that there were many cities in the United States where he could not race because of his color.

efforts to keep blacks from racing, or to at least keep them from winning when they did.

The L.A.W., which regarded itself as a liberal organization, had skirted the racial problem in cycling for several years, but the issue was headed for confrontation. In the early 1890s, chapters in Boston were permitted to enroll blacks as they chose, and southern chapters, which were growing and gaining in influence, were permitted to exclude them. But by 1894, the southern faction forced the League to take a stand, which it did by barring black people from membership nationwide. In a complex exercise

in ambiguity, the L.A.W. did not go so far as to expel individuals already enrolled. Furthermore, it allowed blacks to race in L.A.W.-sanctioned races as long as local chapters approved.

This was the situation when an ex-racer and bicycle entrepreneur named Birdie Munger offered to take Major Taylor under his wing and make him, as he said, "the fastest bicycle rider in the world." Indeed, the teenager was showing promise. The year after his forced debut in racing, he won another local road race and came home with the prize of a vacant lot, which he promptly gave to his mother. In 1896, he entered a six-day at Madison Square Garden. He did this against the advice of people who said nothing broke down a racer like the single six, but he did well enough in New York to increase his reputation. A black rider on any racing circuit at the time was a novelty, and novelty was what the promoters of this booming sport sought.

Munger and Taylor moved to Worcester, Massachusetts, where Munger opened a factory to produce bicycles as well as manage Taylor's career in a less racially hostile atmosphere. Later in 1896, Taylor joined the professional circuit and raced within inches of "Cannon" Bald, Tom Cooper, Nat Butler, and many other top riders. Major Taylor became a favorite of cycle fans, and he began to earn good money, often $150 for a

day's work. In Philadelphia that year, at races connected with the L.A.W.'s annual convention, he made the finals of the mile sprint and took a strong fourth to Earl Kiser, Bald, and Cooper.

The next year Taylor was a serious rival wherever he raced. Predictably, there came accusations of conspiracies among other riders to keep Taylor from winning and causing them the embarrassment of being defeated by a black man. A common tactic at the time was to "pocket" a rider, or keep him hemmed in, and throw elbows and other fouls his way. This was a continuing problem for Taylor throughout his career. Evidence was that he gave as well as he got, and he was never too shy to argue his case before judges, who were often unsympathetic. But from the beginning of his career, there was something stoic about Taylor,

1899 Victor Chainless Overman Cycle Co., Chicopee Falls, Massachusetts
Racing was behind the development and promotion of the chainless. In 1897, Columbia came out with its "bevel-gear" shaft drive, which sold reasonably well. The Victor version of the chainless shaft-driven machine used a "spin roller" which had small rollers on the teeth to lessen the friction that presumably slowed the Columbia. This was a very well-engineered bicycle, but its designers had reason to claim it never got a fair test on the open market. The year the Victor Chainless was introduced, the once-mighty Overman Cycle Company left the bicycle business.

Marshall "Major" Taylor prospered very well as a bicycle racer. Here he poses proudly with his wife Daisy and their daughter Sydney, who was three years-old in 1908 when this photo was taken in Paris. Sydney was named for the city in Australia, where she was born during Taylor's wildly successful racing tour of that country in 1903-04.

who never lashed out and who often backed off when racial hostility turned too intense.

Despite such obstacles, 1897 was a good year for Taylor. He was among the leading point-getters on the professional circuit and might have had a good chance of finishing the year as the nation's top rider. But that was before the pro tour swung to the South, where Taylor could not race without dire risks to his personal safety. Thus, he ended the year well down in the rankings.

The next year, the professional race circuit began with intense public interest in seeing Major Taylor race, and he was stronger than ever. Naturally, there were racial tensions. In Philadelphia, a promoter announced that he was barring Taylor from races at his track, based on his interpretation of L.A.W. policy, which barred black people from membership. The uproar in Philadelphia, however, caused the promoter to back off and let Taylor race. "The promoter who would debar a good drawing card like Major Taylor does not understand his business," the promoter finally said. Major Taylor went on to win major races that year at New York's Manhattan Beach, New Jersey's Asbury Park, and other large tracks. He was routinely jostled by other riders, but after big wins that fall at another race in Philadelphia—in the 1/3-mile and 2-mile distances—his rivals showed up in his dressing room to congratulate him.

Problems did not end, of course. Later in 1898, most top professionals dropped out of the L.A.W. and joined the new National Cycling Association, which now sanctioned and promoted pro races. This move was made partially to enable pros to race on Sundays, a practice the L.A.W. prohibited. Sunday racing was a distinct problem for Taylor, because he was a devout Baptist who had vowed to his late mother never to race on the Sabbath. There were intimations that the N.C.A.'s secret agenda was to eliminate Taylor from its field, which it largely did.

At any rate, bicycle racing was peaking in popularity, and there was still money to be made. The public was clamoring for speed and more speed, and many promoters found that one way to draw paying crowds was to stage paced match races. "Pacing" meant that the competitors were led by teams on tandems, triplets, quadruplets, and even sextuplets to set the pace and break wind resistance. It was an irresistibly exciting event when two top racers competed over distances up to twenty-five miles, and Major Taylor became a main attraction in these events at tracks throughout the East. His first major victory in a match of this sort was against Welsh professional Jimmy "Midget" Michael. The Major earned $1,000 for the victory at the Manhattan Beach track, and he was now winning international acclaim.

Pacing also attracted manufacturers who sponsored racers with an opportunity to demonstrate their increasingly powerful "multicycles." Waltham Manufacturing Company, an important Taylor sponsor in this period, invested heavily in pacing machines, which it hoped to sell on the market along with its lightweight racing bicycles. There was nothing overly complex about multicycles, except that sprockets increased in size from front to back, as the first rider assisted the pedaling of the second, the second assisted the third, and so on. The most important quality was strength—of the machine as well as of the riders. A good five-seater typically used 1-1/8-inch diameter steel tubing. Waltham's Oriten (an anagram of the company's Orient model), a ten-seater, used 1-1/2-inch tubing and weighed 300 pounds.

While the featured rider on his 18-pound racer got all the glory, the team on the multicy-

RIGHT: The chainless concept was relatively simple, and manufacturers hoped that it would provide ample reason for experienced cyclists to trade in their old machines and step up to the new technology. While most major manufacturers introduced a chainless in the last half of the 1890s, it never did displace chain-drive.

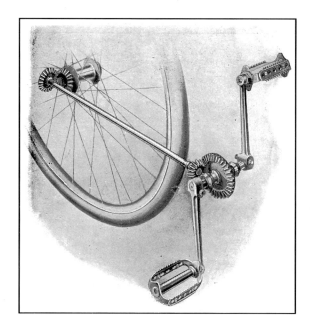

BELOW: The Orient Chainless, like many chainless bicycles, did better on the track—especially in long-distance pace racing—than it did on the commercial market. They ran with great smoothness over distances, but lacked the accelerating power of chain-drive cycles. The Orient Chainless was the bicycle ridden by Major Taylor in his prime.

cle was doing some very hard work. Steering in particular was an ordeal. "At a slow pace it required great muscular force to turn the handle-bar at all," wrote a pace rider testing the Oriten for the first time in 1898. And as racing speeds climbed as high as 40 miles per hour, "The wind pressure [was] rather unpleasant, for the steersman [caught] all of it." In sum, this rider concluded in a trade magazi... ...at "If you are looking for a safe, soft and easy job, pass multi-

cycling by. You'll find shoveling sand very much easier, and considerably safer, too."

Paced racing was also suited to another developing technology , the chainless drive shaft. Chainless technology had been around in various forms, but by 1897 the drive shaft was sufficiently advanced for a model to be produced and sold by Pope Manufacturing. The Columbia chainless used beveled gears in an enclosed system and could be "taken apart and put together by any person of ordinary intelligence," according to its advertising.

Chainless bicycles made a mark in racing—widely considered the testing ground for legitimate bicycle technology—the following year when a mechanic named Harry Sager replaced the teeth of the gears with "roller pins" in a device that reduced friction. Sager collaborated with the Waltham company and put Major Taylor on one such machine. It was a smooth ride, and was particularly effective for its high gear. The chainless was also a more expensive machine, and any good notice that Taylor could generate for it would be a boon for the manufacturer, who was always looking for ways to entice riders to trade up.

Major Taylor did his part. In solo time trials that fall at Philadelphia's Woodside Park's banked pine-board track, Taylor and his entourage made a focused assault on a series of world time records, including the most coveted record in America, the one-mile "flying start." To achieve it, the Waltham people and Sager assembled the best quintuplet pacers in the business. Taylor quickly established world records in distances ranging from the quarter-mile to two miles. But in the flying-start mile, added interest was generated when the sponsors offered Taylor an additional $10,000 if he could break the 1 minute 30 second mark. Taylor got the world record but couldn't get the $10,000, though he was never shaken from the pace and could be heard shouting at his quintuple for more speed. "It was evident to everyone that no human pace is fast enough for him," wrote the *Philadelphia Press*.

This led to the next logical development: steam- and gas-powered pacers, which in turn marked the beginning of an entirely new industry, motorcycles. It was hardly a smooth transition. In the first big paced event of 1899, a match between Taylor on his Waltham chainless and Eddie McDuffie on his Columbia

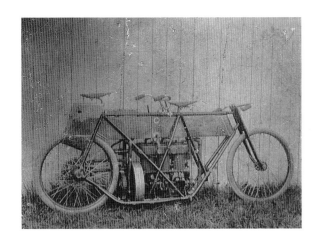

chainless was arranged for a distance of 15 miles, purse of $1,000. Adding to the natural excitement of the event was the fact that it was to be the first big match race where pacers had motors. It was not a success, unfortunately, as McDuffie's steam cycle spewed and sputtered posing great risk to the riders. The 10,000 spectators assembled for the race went away disappointed, though they had a good laugh.

Motorcycles had not developed as reliable pacing vehicles before one of the most spectacular events ever in cycling took place in 1899. It was the stupendous feat of "Mile-a-Minute Murphy," Charles M. Murphy of Brooklyn, who rode on a smooth-board track behind a train

LEFT: The search for speed on bicycles gave rise to the next step in transportation technology: motorcycles. This one featured three cylinders and two riders (one to steer and the other to control the throttle) and paced a former high-wheel bicycle champion named Peter Berlo of Boston.

BELOW: Mile-a-Minute Murphy earned his name behind this Long Island Railroad train with a specially built hood on its rear. The ties of the track were overlaid with a platform which the daring Murphy nearly overshot at the end of his famous run.

Charlie "Mile-a-Minute" Murphy.

chance to show his mettle against the world class of cycling. This he did by winning the mile championship, after which he made a poignant victory lap with an American flag wrapped around his waist as a sash. "I never felt so proud to be an American before," he wrote, "and indeed, I felt even more American at that moment than I had ever felt in America."

Taylor's triumph in Montreal could be seen as a high point for American bicycling. By 1900, the bicycle boom in this country was in decline, and although bicycle racing of various kinds remained popular for another two or three decades, it would soon share the limelight with motorized toys. Taylor had some good years left, mostly abroad, while in this country, manufacturers who were also sponsors of the sport were going out of business one after another. Perhaps the most telling sign of what was happening in America was that by the end of the Major's career, he was riding a bicycle with a frame built by hand and with components that had all come from Europe.

with a special rear platform to maximize the airfoil. It was madness, and Murphy almost overshot his smooth track—a gory prospect indeed. But this elaborate arrangement allowed him to not just break the record, but obliterate it. He rode a timed mile in 57 seconds. No human-powered vehicle had even contemplated such a feat before.

To the credit of other cyclists of the period, no one tried to replicate the Murphy stunt. Instead, Taylor's handlers and other teams worked the kinks out of the steam- and gasoline-powered pacing vehicles. They continued to break records and make money. But Taylor in particular had other business in 1899. This was the World Championships in Montreal, a competition that had nothing to do with mechanical gimmickry. Because previous world championships had been held on Sundays (most of Europe did not observe the day of rest), Taylor had never before competed in the most prestigious of all meets. The Canadians, however, did observe the Sabbath, and finally Taylor had a

LEFT: In the 1890s, Murphy claimed to have designed this three-roller home trainer which measured his distance with flashing lights. Years later, roller racing became a popular sport in which promoters needed only a theater, not a track, to pit one bicycle racer against another.

As Americans began making names for themselves on the international track-racing circuit, they not only wore their sponsor's name prminently on their chest, they often took their victory laps with an American flag wrapped around the waist. Americans were every bit the racers that Europeans were around the turn of the century. Only later did the English, Dutch, and French leave the Yanks behind—until the 1980s when Greg LeMond amazed the world with his triumphs in the Tour de France.

Chapter Five

The Bicycle Bust

FOR EVERY BOOM— such as the bicycle industry had enjoyed in the 1890s—there follows a bust, which in this case emitted unmistakable signs early on. One symptom was volatile prices. When the "safety bicycle" of the era had reached its engineering standard in 1892 or so, most bicycles cost in the range of $150. This was more than most Americans earned in a month, and whether or not the price reflected the bicycle makers' costs, the popular press often chided them for gouging.

The industry, for the most part, seemed willing to endure the criticism. What upset most bicycle manufacturers, however, was the rise of discounting retailers. In fact, nothing riled the industry during the bicycle boom like news that some compatriots were cutting prices. In 1893, when the Warwick Company, a respectable East Coast store, announced that it was lowering prices on its best bicycle to $85, a howl came from many corners. A columnist for *Outing* magazine—largely supported by Pope and other manufacturers— claimed that such a price was "below all reason." In fact, it might have ignited a bicycle price war then and there, except that '93 was a depression year, a fact which delayed any significant price movement until the economy improved.

In 1895, prices of bicycles came down broadly, to an average of $100. That was enough to expand a boom into a relative craze. The industry projected sales of 400,000 that year (output was

RIGHT: 1900 Pierce Arrow George N. Pierce Co., Buffalo, New York "Tried and True" was the head tag on this machine. The Pierce company shunned the Bicycle Trust, the would-be monopoly of the industry in 1899, which did little but lower quality and suppress innovation. Pierce, on the other hand, made what was probably the best bicycle of this era. It had a shaft drive, which was considered preferable to the chain at this time. State-of-the-art suspension came from a front fork of spring leaves and a telescopic shock absorber on the drop bar. It was called the Pierce Hygienic Cushion Frame with an eye toward its healthful anti-vibration qualities.

Pierce Cycles of Buffalo did not join the American Bicycle Company trust, maintaining its tradition of independence and the highest quality product. The Pierce bicycle was distinguished for effective rear suspension with a hydraulic cylinder at the top of the drop bar. Within a few years the Pierce family began building top-of-the-line motorcycles and automobiles as well.

800,000), and two years later, fully two million bicycles were sold in this country. These numbers suggested that the market was in the throes of something it could not sustain. Indeed, bicycles were being sold in the strangest places, not just in bicycle shops and other special retailers, but at general purpose hardware stores, drug stores, cigar stores, clothing stores, and even saloons.

Downward pressure on prices continued, and it was pressure that the popular press enjoyed augmenting with investigations. The *New York Herald* reported that, based on its analysis, a $100 bicycle actually cost $30 to build, the result of which was enormous profits for manufacturers. This triggered an instantaneous response from the bicycle trade press, which insisted that there were many expenses connected with the selling of a bicycle, not the least of which were advertising and promotions, including the sponsorship of racing teams that seemed to be obligatory for any maker with the least bit of ambition. Costs of advertising really were high in such a fast-expanding market, a fact which seemed to ensure that the market would soon burst. When it did, it was a rude awakening for everyone concerned.

Price Wars and the Trust

There was evidence that the market was starting to saturate as early as 1896, when one new maker of a high-quality machine wrote in its brochure that its product was a "low-overhead" model, meaning that the company spon-

sored no racers and advertised only modestly. The result was a bicycle that was otherwise a good $100 product going for $85. From that time on, price undercutting continued by makers and retailers, despite attempts to establish "fair-trade" agreements, which were signed but largely ignored.

Another time bomb in the market was the fact that by 1896, many new bicycles were actually replacements, sold to people who already owned bicycles but wanted to keep up with improvements. The industry was definitely riding a wave of "planned obsolescence," a practice which generated profits for some of the makers but also created a threat to new-customer sales—the used bicycle market. Used bicycles were a burden to the industry for at least two reasons. First, new model "improvements" were sometimes nothing more than superficial—a change in color or a slightly different rake in the front fork—and used bicycles were often no worse than new ones. A second problem was that whatever reputation would later be garnered by used-car salesmen was already well-deserved by used bicycle salesmen. These factors did nothing to stabilize a market that was looking drunk with success and declining by '98.

While the bicycle boom was endangered for many reasons, many in the industry scrambled to survive. One symptom of the impending bust was the entry of the large department stores into the bicycle market at its height. Mass merchandisers, with their ability to shave prices, began in the market by selling lower grade bicycles, leaving high-grade models to small bicycle shops. Still, as department stores sold hundreds of bicycles every week for less than $50 in many cases, it quickened the saturation of the market.

Troubles in the bicycle kingdom could no longer be ignored when the Overman Wheel Works, which had arguably manufactured the best-built bicycles on the market only a few years before, entered bankruptcy in 1897. For the other manufacturers, it became an effort to survive, and many of them saw the department stores as their last, best chance. The result was better-quality bicycles being sold at ever lower prices. At the end of 1897, with the new 1898 models about to come in, Wanamaker's of New York City sold a storeroom full of $100 machines for $27.50 each.

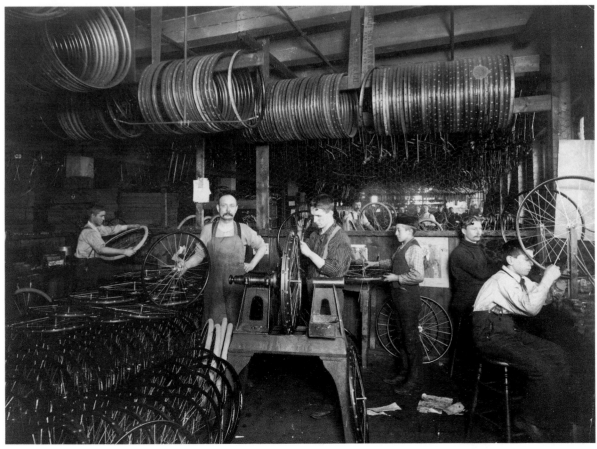

TOP AND BOTTOM: Arnold, Schwinn & Co. of Chicago had many things going for it in the bicycle industry's bleak years. As frame makers they understood the value of heavy-duty durability at a time when the primary market for bicycles was for youngsters. And Ignaz Schwinn knew production, as these early company photographs demonstrate.

Independent bicycle shops and small makers, both of which were important contributors to the industry when it was healthy, could not compete.

Outright shenanigans added to the industry's woes. The Monarch Cycle Manufacturing Company was distressed to discover that a number of low-quality models—produced by Monarch explicitly for export—had appeared in Ludwig Bros. department store in New York,

Bicycle accessories, or "sundries" as they were called, were big business during the boom, and as the market for bicycles turned down, ever-resourceful sundry makers quickly converted their product lines for the next technologies on the horizon. These were motorcycles and automobiles, for which the kerosene lamps of the bicycle were easily adaptable.

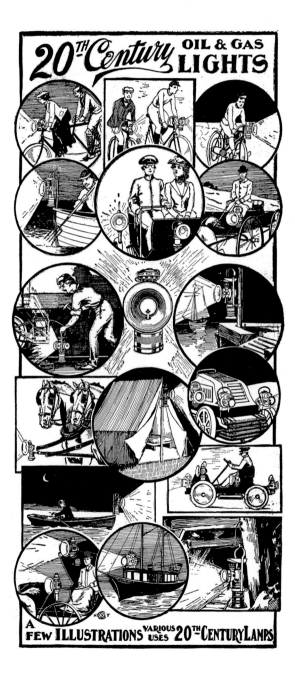

billed as Monarch's top-of-the-line model at a deeply discounted price of $34.50. Monarch sued and received a settlement of $1,000 for damages, but of course this did nothing to expand a seriously oversold market. Another outrage was a practice called "stripping," wherein stores purchased top-quality bicycles from manufacturers, stripped them of first-rate tires, saddles, pedals, and other components, and replaced them with cheaper features. One such retailer, it was reported, refined this practice by stripping $5.00 tires made by Morgan & Wright, probably the best rubber-tire maker, and replacing them with tires that cost $3.00 a pair. The retailer then sold the five-dollar pair for $2.65, scalping an extra profit of $.65.00 cents for each pair sold. This practice was widespread enough that some makers advertised that theirs was "an honest wheel," immune from such brazen fraud.

As the market continued to decline, manufacturers were at a loss. Finally, many determined that if they could not defeat the discounters, they should join them. In 1898, a cartel of makers was formed which signed a contract with a group of major department stores, including the Fair Store of Chicago and Gimbel's of Philadelphia. The cartel agreed to supply of a minimum of 20,000 bicycles to be sold at deeply discounted prices, as low as $13.25. Obviously, the quality of cycles made for this price suffered terribly, and the reputation of the industry continued to plummet.

Efforts were made to save the industry from collapse. In December 1897, the large Cleveland manufacturer H. A. Lozier declared that he simply would not sell his highest-quality bicycles to department stores. In *Cycle Age* magazine he allowed that:

The largest and most reliable department stores have grown thoroughly tired of the cheap trash which the majority of them have sold in the past, and rather than go out of the business entirely they have decided to try high-priced machines on an equal footing with the legitimate dealers . . . Yet it is our opinion that the best of these concerns, if they found that the venture did not pay as they expected, or if they found themselves in a tight place, would not hesitate a moment to cutting prices in two, or anything to unload in a hurry.

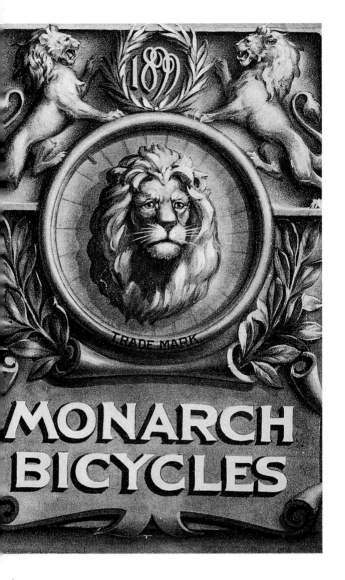

In 1899, a new combine called the American Bicycle Company absorbed many of the nation's hundreds of bicycle makers. Barnes and Monarch were among formerly independent companies that became subsidiaries, and in some cases simply brand names, of the "Bicycle Trust." This effort by Albert Pope and others to monopolize the industry was not a success. Several important makers as well as parts manufacturers remained outside the Trust. Moreover, the would-be monopoly drained the industry of its innovation and customary marketing savvy. The Trust's financial structure collapsed in 1903 when it defaulted on its bonds.

But even while Lozier attempted to maintain his independence in the market, an effort of a different sort to save the once-booming industry was afoot. It was the creation of the huge American Bicycle Company (A.B.C.), the so-called "Bicycle Trust." As was the practice in many other industries at this time, the Trust was an attempt to monopolize trade, control prices, and ensure hefty profits for the manufacturers. Front man for this enterprise was bicycle maker A. G. Spaulding, later the baseball and sporting goods czar, who in 1898 set up an office in a suite at New York's Waldorf-Astoria hotel. There, Spaulding received the owners of many major bicycle companies, and they assembled their would-be monopoly.

By early the next year, the bicycle trust was a reality, composed of Spaulding's firm and those of Pope, Monarch, Gormully & Jeffery, Chicago's huge Western Wheel Works, and, not too surprisingly, Lozier. In all, the A.B.C. controlled an estimated capacity of 653,000 bicycles yearly—an impressive number, though it did not represent the entire industry. The Trust was capitalized at $40 million, a reported half of which was in common stock held by the factory owners, and the other half in preferred and bonds bearing interest of 5 percent. (But this is the simplified version. In fact, the organization and financing of the A.B.C. was secretive and ir-

1900
Rambler
Gormully &
Jeffery
Manufacturing
Co., Chicago,
Illinois
The Rambler
was still a proud
piece of
machinery when
low prices took precedence over
high-quality. Its body featured flared
metal tubing for extra strength at the
joints, which were brazed by
immersion in molten brass. These
techniques continued even after G &
J and Rambler became names of the
American Bicycle Company, or Bicycle
Trust, which was not known for the
best manufacturing technifques in all
of its lines.

regular enough that the New York Stock Exchange refused to list it.)

The Trust was a failure from the outset. For one thing, the component makers refused to be co-opted. Morgan & Wright promptly announced that they would sell tires to all comers, not just to the Trust. Steel tubing was available from domestic and foreign sources. Pedals, rims, handlebars, and everything else needed to assemble a bicycle were also available on the open market. Within a few months of the formation of the A.B.C., it was reported that despite the Trust, independent makers still possessed a capacity to make a million bicycles a year.

There were many reasons why the Trust's monopoly failed. First among them was that American entrepreneurs, and especially the men who designed and produced bicycles, were a feisty and hard-headed lot. Many of them rightly perceived that the Trust had little to do with the industry's traditional values of high quality and innovation.

None of the independents were more opposed than the Iver Johnson Firearms Company, makers of Iver Johnson bicycles, which were promptly advertised as non-A.B.C. machines. "Our Bicycles Are Not Made By A Trust," Iver Johnson declared in large print.

Iver Johnson was originally a gunsmith who began in that business around the time of the Civil War. With a factory in Fitchburg, Massachusetts, and with skill in shaping high-quality steel, the firm took to doing what many other companies were doing profitably in the late 1880s—building high-wheeled bicycles. In 1890, with the advent of the safety bicycle, it began making a private label machine for the J. P. Lovell Arms Co., a sporting goods retailer in Boston. The Lovell Diamond, as this bicycle was called, was a successful model in the early boom years. But in 1895, two things happened. Iver Johnson died, and the Lovell firm simultaneously sought a lower price-point for its bicycle. Perhaps the Lovell people thought they could shake a cheaper model out of Iver's son, Fred, than they ever could have gotten from Iver himself. At any rate, the Johnson firm quit making Lovell Diamonds, and J.P. Lovell moved production to a factory in Maine, where construction was notably shoddy. Cones in hubs, for one, were stamped and not machined.

Drop-out brackets for wheels were no longer forged and braised, but rather cut right out of the frame itself.

As the Lovell Diamond declined, Iver Johnson put its own name on its bicycles, and the mark became notable for high quality. The Johnson factory entered the racing game and became a sponsor of Major Taylor. Sales were good, and even when they dropped off around 1897, the firm still had the luxury of good profits from its gun business. At any rate, the Trust was not the solution that Fred Johnson had envisioned for his family firm. When Spaulding and Pope (who was the real power behind Spaulding) formed their cartel, Iver Johnson's loud resistance was one of many signs that the Trust would soon crumble.

Crumble it did. Almost from the very outset, A.B.C. stock plummeted along with bicycle

When the Trust failed, many of its assets fell to Colonel Pope. Thus old Clevelands, once the product of the Lozier Manufacturing Co. in Ohio, became a trade name of Pope Manufacturing, as did the Westfield mark. Ramblers and Sterlings, also in the Trust, eventually came to Pope as well. It seems that the most forward-thinking person from the bicycle-boom days was Thomas Jeffery of Gormully & Jeffery which made Rambler bicycles. G & J joined the Trust, but Jeffery himself dropped out. In 1900, he bought the old Sterling bicycle plant in Kenosha, Wisconsin, and started a new Jeffery enterprise with his son. The result was Rambler cars and the beginnings of what would ultimately became American Motors Corporation.

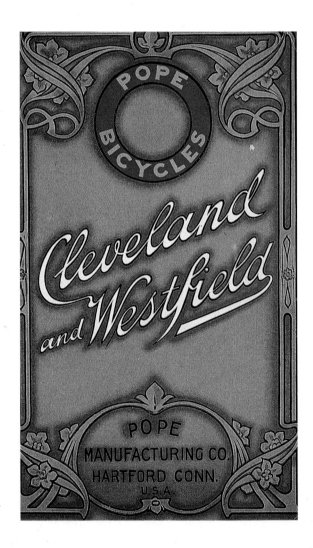

prices. *Bicycling World,* one of the journals once controlled by firms like Pope's, took special delight in announcing that "the securities of the American Bicycle Co. continue to sag pitifully. The common stock is quoted around 13, the preferred at about 43, while even the supposed gilt-edged bonds hover around 86 with no recorded purchases at these figures." The enterprise was doomed. Within a year, Chicago's Western Wheel Works exited the Trust, then reentered. In 1901, the treasurer of the Trust resigned and bought five of the factories therein in an attempt to form his own trust. The following year, the whole enterprise was held above water and eventually purchased by Albert Pope, with help from his friend, cycling enthusiast John D. Rockefeller. In 1903, A.B.C. bonds were in default.

The Bicycle Trust was clearly a flawed concept that would be outlawed shortly thereafter by federal anti-trust legislation written by the Teddy Roosevelt administration. The Trust was only a symptom, however, of a more widespread malaise in the bicycle industry. The great marketing boom was probably over well before the formation of the Trust. That was because, when price-cutting became rampant, the first thing that makers eliminated was lavish advertising. With the loss of advertising came the loss of press support. Newspapers moved bicycling news to their back pages. The *Bulletin of the League of American Wheelmen* went out of business shortly after the Trust suspended all advertising; Spaulding and Pope reasoned that the journal was unnecessary for a monopoly, even though the monopoly was never to materialize.

Bicycles Sprout Motors

Of course, the most important impediment against continued prosperity in the bicycle industry was another creature of the industry itself: motorized vehicles. Clearly, the public was irresistibly drawn to the next great invention on the horizon. In this case, it was the "motorcycle," a term that for a few years encompassed two-, three-, and four-wheeled conveyances with engines. The next chapter in the history of cycling was near, and it was the story of attaching motors to contraptions that had been previously drawn by the muscles of men and beasts.

Among the motorcar and motorcycle makers, not unexpectedly, were erstwhile bicycle manufacturers. Prominent among them were the Duryea brothers, Charles and J. Frank, whose names are central to the history of the automobile. The Duryeas, Charles in particular, had been granted numerous bicycle patents in the 1880s and 90s, and enjoyed modest success with a safety bicycle called the Duryea Sylph, featuring a unique spring frame with a cushioned fork. Other innovations to their credit included a new saddle, a liquid tire-sealing product called Neverleak, and an early dropped frame, which encouraged more women to ride. (Charles was active in women's rights issues, and while living in Washington he taught America's first female lawyer, Belva Lockwood, how to ride a bicycle.)

The Duryeas were better and more passionate bicycle inventors than they were busi-

"Built Like a Watch"

The Sterling Bicycle

THE POPE MANUFACTURING COMPANY
HARTFORD, CONN., U. S. A.

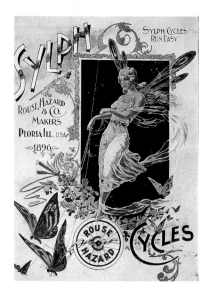

Sylph bicycles were originally the creation of Charles Duryea in 1888. They were early safety bicycles with various innovations in suspension, such as spring frames and cushion forks, and Duryea continued to develop new features for the bicycle which he successfully patented, but marketed with limited success. Duryea, who worked closely with his brother Frank, went on to develop internal combustion engines and carriages that could run under their power. By the turn of the century, Duryea set up the Duryea Power Company and built America's first production automobile, turning out a car a week for the next seven years. Meanwhile, an Illinois company that also had the Overland bicycle added the Sylph to its line.

nessmen. Thus, they left little of pecuniary value behind when they moved on to experiments in internal combustion and automobile mechanics. (It should be noted that Charles was also deeply interested in flying machines and had written a graduate thesis on the subject.) Their work led to the brothers' founding of separate automobile companies in 1898 and 1900. The most successful of these was the Duryea Power Company, which produced one car per week between 1900 and 1907. The Duryeas were quickly overshadowed by others in the automobile industry, but they are considered the true pioneers of American-manufactured, gas-powered cars.

Perhaps more important to the history of bicycles in this period was the development of motorcycles. Efforts to rig steam engines to bicycles actually went back decades, well before the bicycles or the motors were ready for such a commercial marriage. As early as the 1860s, reasonably successful prototypes had been built, though none had been put into production, for reasons of both safety and cost. Then, in 1894, with the bicycle industry nearing its peak, an inventor and promoter named Pennington began attending trade shows with a motorized machine that appeared to be light, powerful, and affordable.

There were some obvious problems with the Pennington, however, even on its face. The most obvious was the fact that it had no cooling mechanism. This was no obstacle for Pennington, since his primary objective, as it turned out, was to run the machine for a few minutes in demonstrations and attract investors to his enterprise. He did rather well at this, explaining briefly to doubters that the ignition of the fuel mixture by electric spark, a rather unknown principle at the time, produced a "refrigerating" effect, and handled all chores of cooling. Predictably enough, the Pennington never went into production. But its inventor was successful at raising considerable capital, after which he disappeared, leaving gullible investors with a raft of debts and a worthless invention.

The first production motorcycle on record was the 1898 Waltham Orient, produced by the Waltham Manufacturing Co., which was at that time sponsoring Major Taylor. Waltham motorcycles began as pacers for bicycle racers in quest

of time records. When Major Taylor declared that what was really needed for new records was a faster vehicle to pace him, Charles H. Metz, owner and inventive genius of Waltham, concocted a motorized tandem, with the front man steering and the rear man controlling the engine. This success soon inspired Metz to assemble a motorized product that might be sold. He chose a four-cycle internal combustion engine, a French-made De Dion that was designed for this purpose, and attached it to a bicycle with an early version of balloon tires.

Waltham's Orient motorcycle was unwieldy, using a 12-pound coil to produce a spark. But as it reached production in 1902—with a 2-1/4-horsepower engine, 5-quart gas tank, and a price tag of $250—the motorized age reached an important milestone. The Waltham firm gave up bicycles the following year.

The most important bridge between the bicycle boom of the 90s and the automobile age to follow was a young mechanic who began his mechanical career working on racing bicycles in Michigan. This mechanic initially showed much skill in tuning and maintaining bicycles, but in time he demonstrated that his real interest was in working with the motorized pacers. He could not get them out of his mind. His name was Henry Ford.

Ford was one of many bicycle mechanics who believed early on that there was commercial promise in the motor, and in 1899 he basically left bicycles to form the Detroit Automobile Company with a group of friends. In 1902, he left that firm to form his own company, which would begin by focusing on race cars and go on to sell production models based on the good publicity garnered from winning. Ford's financial backer was Tom Cooper, a bicycle racer just past his prime who was still regarded as the richest man in the sport. The initial result of Ford's efforts was a racing car which he named the Model 999 (after the most powerful locomotive of the day). The Ford-Cooper car was a 3,000-pound contraption steered with handlebars like a bicycle's.

Cooper was very interested in automobiles, but he was less than enthusiastic about the Model 999. In October 1902, Ford scheduled a race against the Winton Bullet, a Cleveland-made machine that had cornered a major share of the automobile market at this time. Cooper was scheduled to drive, but after a test run around the track at Grosse Pointe, Michigan, he decided that discretion was the better part of valor. The Model 999 had four large cylinders, each the size of a powder keg, it was said, and the whole thing roared with sufficient ferocity to give the normally iron-nerved Cooper pause.

At any rate, Cooper did not drive that day. Instead, Ford's mechanic, a young chap named Barney Oldfield who had never driven before, took the handlebars and won the race. Cooper was soon to leave the partnership. The next year, Oldfield set a world speed mark of 59.6 miles per hour at the Indianapolis Fair Grounds. It was the beginning of several great careers. Indianapolis became the racing capital of the nation. Oldfield was America's first great racer. And Henry Ford, ex-bicycle mechanic, became one of the most important industrialists of the century.

The Spectacle of "Team Sixes"

While bicycles were turning to bust as an industry, cycling was still flying rather high as a sport. Racing was no longer the pastime of the wealthy as it had been in the Hendee and Zimmerman days. Moreover, America's share of triumphs in large international competition had dropped off after the retirement of Major Taylor and his contemporaries. But even as the bourgeoisie moved to other pastimes, cycle racing remained a popular and money-making spectacle. And there was nothing that excited the masses quite like the blood and guts of the six-day.

Six-day racing now was a sanitized version of what it was in the old days, when it was a one-man affair and the sheer exhaustion of the single rider seemed inhuman, which had caused it to be banned. Now the event was for "team sixes," with two men sharing the riding duties Monday through Saturday. As six-day racing brought enormous crowds, venues such as velodromes in Newark and the Bronx became nationally famous. Arenas such as the new Madison Square Garden, built in 1925, and Chicago Stadium, built in 1929, would later make names for themselves primarily because they became important stops for the six-days.

OPPOSITE PAGE RIGHT: By 1910, most manufacturers understood that comfort, not scorching, was all-important in bicycles. This meant a heavier design for many machines—which sometimes bore a resemblance to motorcycles—a longer wheel base, and in Pope's case, an improved "spring fork" which prefigured later efforts toward more elaborate suspension of the bicycle's front end.

BELOW: Six-day races were said to make riders old before their time. But the flowers and cups that came to the winners—riders Lands and Petri are shown here after their triumph at a major six-day in Chicago in 1926—brought weary smiles in those few moments between the finish of a race and a good night's sleep.

one thing, the track was a tight oval, with banks that were as steep as 45 degrees around the turns. And the promoters loved to feature villains, who helped to fill the stands with booing and hissing fans.

One so-called villain of the 1910s and 20s was an Australian named Alf Goullet, known as one of the fastest men on a bicycle. Goullet was aggressive and hard to beat in six-day events, which numbered more than a dozen a year in their heyday. When newspapers picked him as the antagonist of these protracted dramas, promoters did not complain. "That dark and sinister villain, Alfred Goullet, held again the center of the stage last night in the six-day cycling drama at Madison Square Garden," wrote the *New York Times* as it covered a major six-day in 1920. Fans cried out in disgust, which was ironic, because no one was more gentlemanly off the track than "Goullie," as his many friends called him.

But drama brought crowds and enabled promoters to pay top riders like Goullet $1,000 a day to appear, plus whatever they could win of the purse and "premes" (short for premiums) that were announced intermittently over the public address system in the course of the six-day. Premes were sometimes given for a sprint of one mile, other times for ten, and always brought fans to their feet. They were good advertising for companies. Radio manufacturers, liquor companies, and many others got good publicity when the public address speaker called out an award: "Fifty dollars and a box of three fine Arrow shirts, America's favorite shirt, will go to the winner of the next two-mile sprint," the announcement might have declared.

In the evening, these stakes got higher, with actors and actresses offering $200 and more for impromptu sprints. Sprints took their toll on riders who were also racking up laps to try to win the purse for final distance. (Distances were often some 2,500 miles, and if a single mile separated first place from second, it was considered a rout.) But when someone like

Bicycling became great entertainment. It was not out of character for John Ringling, the circus impresario, to be involved as an investor in velodromes in the New York area. Racing veterans today bridle when six-day races are compared to anything like Roller Derby or professional wrestling, but there were parallels. For

upgrade products. Schwinn was particularly irritated by the poor quality of tires, which were little more than "a glorified piece of garden hose," he said. They were tubeless, normally irreparable, and it was considered an advantage to get a large puncture rather than a small one, so the rider would not be tempted into patching the thing, which was normally futile. This problem, of course, served the tire manufacturer nicely, as the replacement market was steady.

As a solution, Schwinn looked to a recent innovation in motorcycles: the "balloon tire" with separate inner tube and wire bead around the edge of the outer tube. This was a far more durable good than what was currently being used, and Frank W.—who had been running the motorcycle division until it was closed—brought the idea to his rubber suppliers. They dismissed it "as a silly idea," Schwinn remembered.

So Schwinn went to Germany, where balloon tires had been in use in a healthy bicycle industry for some years. He brought back a load of two-inch tire sets and put them on metal rims. With this as a starting point, Schwinn mechanics then built a wider and more solid frame with heavier-gauge steel and a double crossbar. These heavy-framed bicycles were assembled and launched on the market in 1933. They began an authentic revolution in the industry.

Inauspiciously called the "B-10E," this new Schwinn was sturdy enough, the market quickly found, to stand up to the abuse of the most incorrigible children. Chain stores, predictably, wanted nothing new or different and refused to stock the new Schwinn. But it sold very nicely through the independent dealers—small bicycle shops on the back alleys of cities and towns that were known to provide better service and a better-adjusted product. They were willing and able to carry a bicycle that cost a few dollars more, but which they knew was far superior to typical chain-store fare.

The B-10E was an enormous success, and before 1933 was over, the entire industry was talking about the relatively abscure bicycle firm in Chicago that had rarely used its own name on its bicycles. Within two years the company not only brought almost the entire industry to the balloon tire, but it made the wording on its nameplate, "Schwinn-built," a mark of considerable prestige. In the years to come, Schwinn would set the standard for style and for quality in American bicycles. Balloon-tire bicycles were one of the most important milestones for one of the most important industrial success stories of the era.

Streamlined Design

Chicago was the site of another important event for the industry at this time. The Century of Progress Exposition on the city's lakefront began in the summer of 1933. It was Chicago's second world's fair and represented America's greatest celebration of Art Deco design. For several years already, the streamlined profile of architecture, machines, clothing, and nearly anything else had been the height of fashion. Art Deco first appeared in 1925 at the Exposition Internationale des Arts Decoratifs et Industriels Modernes in Paris, a fair billed as the apotheosis of machine-made goods. Glass, plastics, sheet metal, and other ultra-smooth surfaces—all in the brightest colors—dazzled Paris visitors who were otherwise accustomed to tired classical designs.

1937 Evinrude Streamflow Evinrude Motors, Milwaukee, Wisconsin
It seemed natural for a precision engineering company like Evinrude to enter the burgeoning bicycle market in 1937. Evinrude designers came up with what they called "the greatest advance in modern bicycle construction." In fact, it was a brilliantly styled piece of work combined with curious innovations in suspension, such as a hinged crank hanger and chain stay assembly which moved up and down independent from the rest of the frame. Evinrude was ready to promote this and subsequent models with its customary zeal, but when early Streamflow frames broke under normal use, the company decided to cut its losses and get out of the bicycle business.

1938 Ladies' Columbia
Columbia Manufacturing Co.,
Westfield, Massachusetts
In 1938, Columbia was still the most famous name in American bicycles. But the adult market, on which old Col. Pope had made the company's name, was meager, and the early lightweight touring bicycles which Columbia introduced in the 1910s found little market at all. By 1938, Columbia was following the trend for balloon-tire cruisers. This one was deluxe, with a two-speed internal gear in the rear hub and skirt lacing on the rear fender.

The Depression soon arrived, but by 1933, Chicagoans showed a fitful determination to overcome it. Thus, A Century of Progress represented an opportunity for the industrial world to show how far it had come and where it was going. Transportation was an obvious theme, and Henry Ford invested more than one million dollars in an exhibit for his automobiles, now sleeker and emphatically aerodynamic. Another demonstration of the 1933 fair featured the Buckminster Fuller's Dymaxion Car. It was described as a "first-stage experimental vehicle leading to eventual omni-medium wingless transport." Its description may have bewildered, but its tear-drop form of aluminum and

chrome-molybdenum could go 120 miles per hour. Unfortunately, a fatal crash shortly after the fair garnered negative publicity for Fuller and scotched development of his car. But streamlined design was here to stay.

Frank Schwinn liked to say that the bicycle industry "got religion" in 1933. Religion, in this case, was the impulse to innovate and promote. The Cycle Trades Association apologized to its members in 1933 when it offered only a paltry exhibit in the exposition's Transportation Building. Then, when fair promoters announced plans to remain open a second year, the industry association was ready with a larger and far more impressive installation. This featured historic bicycles to

—16"—

The problem was, of course, that most balloon-tire models looked better than they rode. According to Frank W. Schwinn:

The female star was always on the front page news. The publicity magnified the actual interest a thousandfold—made people somewhat cycle conscious, particularly women and girls who wanted to reduce—and brought about the cycle rental business which flared up and died down again over a period of about five years. Many adults rented and rode bicycles, a few bought bikes, but very few. There was a reason. The bikes were heavy, cumbersome toys with which children could bump curbstones and not break up.

As a means of adult transportation or even casual enjoyment, they needed work.

Still, Frank Schwinn was determined to develop the adult market. As the Depression waned, he made another trip to Europe, where bicycles were a part of everyday life. Schwinn's goal was to understand the technology and marketing of the machines that were called "lightweights." He later said that even the trip caused ridicule among colleagues in industry—

they remained infuriatingly conservative. But he persevered, and took to calling himself "the heretic" for his determination to make the bicycle market turn another corner. Schwinn returned from his European sojourn with more than a dozen French and English lightweights, along with spare rims, hubs, cranks, and other components that were manufactured with a level of lightness and quality that was unimagined by most U.S. manufacturers of this time.

Schwinn believed he could build a bicycle equal to, if not better than, the best that Europe offered. To figure out how, he visited an old friend named Emil Wastyn in Wastyn's bicycle shop on Chicago's West Side. Emil was an immigrant from Belgium who had come to this country in 1910. He'd immediately jumped into bicycle building, and, along with Pop Brennan in New Jersey, became one of the greatest cycle mechanics of his era. He built racers for famous six-day riders such as Jimmy Walthour and Al Crossley, who formed one of the greatest teams ever. Other big-name riders—Cecil Yates, Jerry Rodman, Bobby Thomas, to name a few—rode the six-day circuit with at least two "Wastyns" in tow.

c. 1950s Black Phantom
Arnold, Schwinn & Co.,
Chicago, Illinois
For reasons which had as much to do with the baby boom as this bicycle's intrinsic design, the Black Phantom become one of the most popular bicycles ever in America. It had a curvaceous cantilever frame, a refinement of the streamlining that had been going on for nearly two decades. It had the knee-action spring fork, a fine-looking feature even if it did not conquer every pothole on postwar American roads. It had a cycle lock and the added attraction of a guarantee against theft for a year. Most of all, it had chrome—on rims, tank, fenders and wherever else it could be added. Chrome made heavy bikes look faster than they were.

ponents from B.S.A., also in England. A Wastyn, therefore, was no stock production model. Most were custom-made and measured precisely to the individual racers who ordered them. The rider's inseam dictated frame height. A long torso indicated that the saddle should be adjusted back. A Wastyn "racing stem" was adjustable forward or back, though Emil could also fabricate a solid stem from light, drop-forged steel. The Wastyn racer weighed around 18 pounds, and racers swore by them.

It was Schwinn's desire to put something on the market that at least resembled one of those fine, Wastyn-built machines. Fortunately, Schwinn was successful enough in his lesser lines to do just that and make an investment in a new American bicycle "out of all proportion to possible return," he later stated without re-

ABOVE: The Paramount came about in 1938 when Frank W. Schwinn and master bicycle maker Emil Wastyn collaborated to build a bicycle that was as race-ready as any European machine at the time. Chrome-moly tubing and European components suddenly put an American manufacturer in the forefront of racing bicycles, though it would take some time before those unprofitable efforts translated into lightweight sales.

RIGHT: 1952 J.C. Higgins Regal Deluxe Color Stream
Sears, Roebuck & Co.,
Chicago, Illinois
By 1952, bicycles had established themselves as true neighborhood status symbols. Thus, the line that was named after Sears, Roebuck's first accountant, Mr. Higgins, was "so streamlined with its modern design and fresh, gay color combination, that it is a standout anywhere," according to the Sears catalog. Some nice features of this bike were an abundance of reflectors, an elaborate skirt guard on this ladies' model, and a Batwing headlight. (Note: Most surviving Color Streams lack the headlight because the cell batteries required were heavy and caused spills while the bike was parked, thus breaking the headlight.) Price was $59.95, less than one dollar a pound for this 70-pound dazzler.

When Schwinn trundled home from Europe with his load of French and English hardware, Wastyn was more than familiar with all of it. He already was stocking the best materials and parts available—Reynolds tubing from England; cranks, sprockets, hubs, and other com-

gret. Thus, with Wastyn's design expertise and Frank W.'s money, Arnold, Schwinn & Co. came out with the Schwinn Paramount in 1938. It was probably the most important American bicycle that did not turn a cent in profit. It also marked an audacious beginning

for a new category of American bicycles: light-weights. "The most advanced thought and practice in modern design, engineering, precision workmanship and metallurgy" was how the company described the genesis of the Paramount line. It was hardly an exaggeration.

For the first time ever, an American bicycle factory produced frames of chrome-molybdenum, an alloy originally developed for military aircraft use. Hubs and axles were machined of the finest hardened steel. Crank sets were chrome moly as well. The retail price was $75, high for the time but not outlandish. Still, there was a sense among other makers and even people inside his own company that Frank Schwinn's efforts to nudge the bicycle industry forward were nothing but a pipe dream. But if

Schwinn ever entertained doubts about this project, he needed only to stop at Emil Wastyn's on his way home. They would discuss the many details of high-performance cycling, such as racing grips, the ideal curvature of the front fork, and the prospect of light metal rims soon replacing the wooden ones still preferred by racers.

Schwinn, along with Wastyn, believed that the Paramount was at least as good as the best bicycle in the world. But how to prove it? The answer, they decided, lay in events that had taken place some forty years before, when classic racers such as Major Taylor had won fame not just for great victories over other riders, but for their regular attempts at setting world time records. Schwinn and Wastyn remembered the

1952 Roadmaster Luxury Liner
Cleveland Welding Co.,
Cleveland, Ohio
One of the first industrial designers to utter the words "planned obsolescence" was Brook Stevens who designed this Roadmaster. His meaning was "better, more desirable products each season so customers can't resist upgrading." In this case it meant a Shockmaster coiled-spring front fork, chrome-trimmed horn tank, rear carrier with taillights, and a Searchbeam headlight which was unusually powerful and tempted kids to stay out after dark.

Paced racing was mostly a thing of the past, but Schwinn reckoned that something like it might bring much-needed notice to the Paramount. He began talking to Wastyn about an attack on not just a speed record but the unheard-of bicycle speed barrier of 100mph. Wastyn said that he could build a Paramount that could go for the mark. They also believed they could find a motor vehicle of some sort to pace it. But who would ride?

The choice, in retrospect at least, was obvious. Alfred Letourner, the "Red Devil," as he was called, was considered one of the gutsiest six-day riders on the circuit. Born and reared in France, Letourner exploded on the American scene in 1931 when he won the first Madison Square Garden race he entered (with teammate Marcel Guimbretiere). He had strength and leg speed; he also had daring, a fact which was eminently clear every time he cut low from a

ABOVE: 1953 Monark Holiday
Monark Silver King, Inc.,
Chicago, Illinois
Many of the elaborate features on the Holiday had become standard in the cruiser age of bicycles. However, the use of wood trim—common on automobiles—was rather unusual on a bicycle.

RIGHT: Alfred Letourner, one of the top six-day racers of the era, traveled to Bakersfield, California, and on May 17, 1941, rode in the draft of a specially equipped midget racer to achieve the amazing speed of 108.92 miles per hour. The feat was sponsored by Schwinn, and Letourner rode a Paramount with a gear ratio of 9-1/2 to 1. It was a credit to Emil Wastyn, who built the bicycle, that Letourner would even attempt such a feat on a machine that weighed a scant 20 pounds. But Wastyn was one of the most trusted names in bicycles, as was Schwinn, and Letourner was the daredevil who made cycling history.

motor pacers—early motorcycles—which provided a draft for the cyclists, and how the top riders had claimed that the only thing that kept them from still faster times was a faster pacer.

banked turn to break free from even the tightest jams. But daring even greater than this would be necessary for the speed record that the bicycle makers had in mind. Although Le-

tourneur had ridden behind motor pacers before, this time would be different.

The Paramount that Schwinn and Wastyn built for Letourner had an enormous front sprocket which almost touched the ground, and a gear ratio of 9-1/2 to 1. (Most bikes were 2-1/2 to 1.) To pace it they got a midget race car and outfitted it with airfoil and a small roller behind that almost touched the pavement (a safety measure in case the rider drew too close).

Letourner's attempt was made on May 17, 1941, on a remote stretch of pavement near Bakersfield, California. The track was more than eight miles long and nearly as flat as a tabletop. The driver was midget-car racer and former bicycle competitor Ronney Householder. After discussing strategy, Letourner and Householder decided that they would work their way up to the 100mph mark gradually. On their first serious time trial, the speedometer of the pace auto reached the high 90s—enough for a record, to be sure, but still short of the goal. During a break, Letourner told Householder and the timing officials (from the American Automobile Association) that it would take him three miles to reach to full speed, and then four miles to safely slow down. With that, the electronic timers were set up in the fourth mile. Letourner's next try was timed at 97.85mph.

Later that day, Letourner returned to the starting line. He told Householder to be wide open this time at least one mile before they reached the timers. It worked, and when Letourneur reached the end of his next run, his handlers were hooting with glee. His timed mile was an almost unbelievable record: 108.92mph.

Everyone and everything involved got enormous publicity from Letourner's feat, not least Schwinn and the Paramount. It was pointed out that the Paramount was not just fast, but it could withstand the punishment of such speeds. As if to emphasize the point—and the remarkable durability of the hardware—the real record-setting bicycle was kept intact, along with the tires, which were nearly torn to shreds from the heat generated by such high speeds.

Whatever momentum the Letourner record might have generated for lightweight bicycles, however, was interrupted by World War II. Now, as in World War I, bicycle manufacturers possessed the machinery for producing many essential war-related parts. The most important work done by these companies was the manufacturing of metal shells for bombs and bazooka rockets, for which light metals, precision machines, and sure craftsmanship possessed by bicycle makers were critical. The industry was also enlisted to make airplane parts (frames for trainers, for example), parts for gun mounts, and chassis for electronic equipment. War work was all-consuming.

When the war began, only one company was permitted by the provisions of the War Powers Act to continue making bicycles—the Westfield Manufacturing Company, makers of the Columbia cycles that were Colonel Pope's old brand. Columbia was the oldest and still one of the best-known names in American cycling, and its prewar product line featured a range of bicycles, including a lightweight model. Columbia lightweights, in fact, went back to 1916, when the company was the first American firm to use the "epicyclic hub gear." This was the critical piece in the "English" three-speeds that became popular later. The epicyclic gear—also known as the internal-gear hub—was first developed in England by the Sturmey-Archer company, later part of Raleigh. The sys-

The war required some changes in the bicycle industry. Most manufacturers produced shells for big guns, frames for light flight trainers, and other military necessities. But the skills that made American bicycles the sturdiest, if not the lightest, in the world did not go away. Women took over the welding chores, and often got to work on bicycles as well.

LEFT: World War II provided bicycle companies, in this case Schwinn, with the opportunity to get back into motorcycles. Whizzers were less than $100 and were light enough for a Dorothy Lamour to negotiate around the studio lot, even in high heels.

tem made use of a series of small but powerful sprockets inside the hub that could be shifted, via cable, from the handlebars.

While Columbia's early lightweight was a good bicycle and could have been improved with little effort, the prevailing American concept of a bicycle in the early 1940s was the heavy, wide-bodied machine with balloon tires and extreme durability. Thus, the government's wartime order was for 25,000 balloon-tire bicycles per year. Norman Clarke, then vice president (and later owner) of Columbia, tried to talk the officers in charge of industrial production into reducing the weight of the standard military-issue bicycle, which was mostly used around military bases stateside. For adult riders,

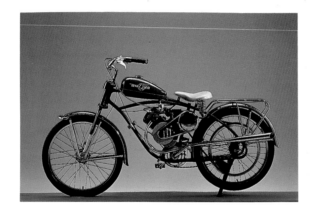

Clarke said, a lighter model, perhaps even a three-speed, would make sense. But this counsel fell on entirely deaf ears, and the company continued producing drab-green klunkers for the duration of the war. (Huffman Manufacturing received some government orders toward the end of the war as well.)

Also rejected during the war years was the notion that bicycles might be used on the battlefield. Discussion of this sort went back a long time. As early as the Spanish-American War, military planners imagined uses for bicycles, and in World War I, prototype bicycles were equipped with gun mounts. Some battlefield use of the bicycle was made by Europeans in the first war, but insofar as Americans were concerned, trench warfare and bicycles were not a logical match, and the machines saw limited action on the Western Front.

Now, in the 1940s, some makers attempted to revive another idea that had been

successfully patented, and unsuccessfully marketed, in the long-past days of the 1890s bicycle boom. This was the folding bicycle, which some believed could be engineered to ride on the backs of paratroopers and provide instant transportation for soldiers dropped behind enemy lines. There was much development work on this idea. Fortunately perhaps, the idea was not carried out, and most airborne troops jumped into Europe unencumbered by such a piece of equipment.

After the technological hiatus of World War II, the postwar era did provide a turning point for American bicycling, or at least the potential for one, in the form of the soldiers returning home. Among their many memories of Europe was one that was positive: the thin-tire bicycles commonly ridden by adults. In England, GIs joined the local people in pedaling around military bases, cities, and towns. More dramatically, stories of the heroic French Resistance often involved men and women riding through enemy lines on bicycles. Now, with the end of the war, European exporters saw an opportunity. In 1946, they sent over nearly 47,000 lightweight bikes, up from 3,600 the year before. Numbers went down the next year, but the influx had made a permanent impact, if not on the buying public, then at least on American bicycle makers. Imports at this time—mostly Raleighs which were England's largest-selling brand—suggested to American companies that a market was there to cultivate.

TOP AND BOTTOM AND NEXT TWO PAGES: In the 1940s, cycle trains got Chicago bicycle clubs out of the city and into the hinterlands for frequent weekend and even week-long trips. The League of American Wheelmen (which included wheelwomen as well) was reborn in this period, and cycling for healthy distances on lightweight bicycles became a regular social activity of many true enthusiasts. These photos are from the collection of Phyllis Harmon of Chicago, one of the hard-core bicyclists during and after World War II. She was later the general secretary of the L.A.W.

The Rise of Touring

There were other reasons to be encouraged about marketing lightweight bicycles to adults. One good sign was the revival of the League of American Wheelmen, which had all but died shortly after World War I when cycling hit a low. The Depression created some new demand for bicycles, especially among young people for whom cars were out of the question. Then as the economy improved, cycling increased modestly and cyclists began to organize themselves again. Many became devoted to their pastime, and sang praises to their escape from the smoke and crowds of industrial cities. Still, their enthusiasm outstripped their numbers considerably.

Even so, the camaraderie of cycling became intense. Wheelmen and wheelwomen

By the postwar period in America, the "epicyclic hub gear," or the typical three-speed, was being brought to America from England and put on American-made bicycles. Caliper brakes were another feature that had been experienced and approved by returning GIs. The problem was that it would take time and serious lobbying in Washington to get any measure of tariff protection for American manufacturers. In fact, Raleighs established themselves in America after the war and never let go of a significant share of the lightweight market.

were quick to form alliances with another social movement of the time, American Youth Hostels, which promoted rugged and simple values. Hostels provided riders with places to stay on the road for a price of twenty-five or thirty cents. Youth hostels also helped assemble groups who would often sing marching songs as they rode on back roads and even pedaled at night, using Swiss-made Lucifer lights and generators (which riders still say were the best ever made).

Chicago was probably the most active cycling center at this time with twenty-three clubs in the area by the early 1940s. Typical of them was the Evanston Cycle Touring Club, which

thought of itself, literally, as being free as the wind. Several times each summer, the Evanston group scheduled "with-the-wind" rides with destinations chosen at the last moment by the direction of the summer breeze. The result was rides which might reach 200 miles in a weekend, after which the club loaded its bicycles on the baggage car of a Chicago-bound train and went home. These resourceful wheelmen and women would even change direction en route if the wind changed.

Because of such active clubs, manufacturers had reason to hope for a real surge in bicycles throughout American society in the postwar period. Still, it did not materialize. The

reason, some said, was once again the bicycle's old nemesis, the automobile. For one thing, the growth of automobile traffic and early development of interstate highways had a bad effect on interurban railway routes, and the "cycle trains" that transported clubs one way or the other grew more rare. Moreover, as automobiles became more abundant and the average wheelbase grew wider, automotive traffic literally squeezed all but the most rabid cyclists off the roads.

The experience of the Evanston club was typical of the time. Because of the danger of cars, roads in town were banned to bicycle riding one by one. Club members did what they

could to write letters and apply political pressure on behalf of bicycles. But it was hopeless. By the mid-1950s, dangers were pronounced, and accidents between bikes and cars were highly publicized. The cars were held mostly blameless. Tickets were written and fines levied against cyclists who rode on streets prohibited to bikes.

American manufacturers faced another obstacle to developing a large market for lightweight bikes: the continued presence of imports. The English, who had invented the three-speed, had a natural edge in this market. Then, in 1949, the pound was devalued from $4.03 to $2.80, and the English product was basically untouchable in this country. European compo-

1957 Corvette
Arnold, Schwinn & Co.,
Chicago, Illinois
The Corvette was the first of Schwinn's middleweight bicycles, developed at a time when heavy cruisers like the Black Phantom seemed obsolete to kids who were now focused on increased speed, or at least the illusion of it. The Corvette had a narrower tire, lighter rims, and other features that took off some of the famous bulk of old "motorbikes." Corvettes and bicycles like them were popular until about 1965 when older baby boomers began adopting more sophisticated touring bikes and racers.

ABOVE, RIGHT, AND NEXT PAGE TOP:
1950 Gene Autry Westerner
Monark Silver King, Inc.,
Chicago, Illinois
It was designed with Gene Autry's
personal involvement, the catalog
claimed. With "rodeo brown" finish,
"jeweled" fenders and chainguard,
and a pony head on the fork crown,
it seemed ready for the silver screen,
if not for the rigors of real life on the
range. Genuine leather holster and
red-handled pistols were standard
equipment. Boys' and girls' bikes
both came in 24-, 20-, and 16-inch
models—for buckaroos and
buckarettes of all sizes.

BELOW: 1959 Wasp
Arnold, Schwinn & Co.,
Chicago, Illinois
The Wasp was marketed to newsboys,
its appeal being its heavy-duty frame
and thick tires—though the trend at
this moment was for thinner and
lighter. Options on this "paper boy
special" included truss rods for more
support, knock-out hubs for easier
maintenance, and heavy-gauge
spokes. However utilitarian, it still
came in radiant colors and did not
look the least bit slow.

nents had the same price advantage, and even
the relatively few American-made lightweights
got many of their components from Europe.

American manufacturers in this period
believed that a market for their own adult bicycles might have gained momentum had the
imported competition faced tariffs of any sub-
stance, but they did not. Postwar Europe, we
must remember, carried an enormous war
debt to the United States, and in Washington
it was considered in the national interest to
encourage those countries to generate whatever foreign-exchange revenue they could.
Thus, duties on foreign bicycles—which also
came from France and even Poland—were
eliminated.

Manufacturers like Norman Clarke, of Columbia Manufacturing, and Frank Schwinn,
among others, made their feelings known at a
series of Congressional hearings on this subject.
They emphasized that as long as the Europeans
dominated adult bicycles, American companies
were powerless in a segment of the market they
believed held potential for them. But the gov-

1953 Juvenile Ranger
Mead Cycle Co., Chicago, Illinois
Among the cowboy entries of the period was this Ranger, a 20-incher for younger kids whose demands on the market led to a cap gun, saddle blanket, and saddle bags, and the ability to ride into the sunset with other Western bikers like Hopalong Cassidy and Gene Autry.

In 1960, Schwinn designed a rocket-inspired bicycle that resembled the Bowden Spacelander. It was never produced, however, as company marketing wizards determined that real speed (read ten-speed racers) and not just the illusion of it was the next trend in cycling. Schwinn focused its efforts on drop handlebars and derailleurs instead. As usual in this period, they were right on target.

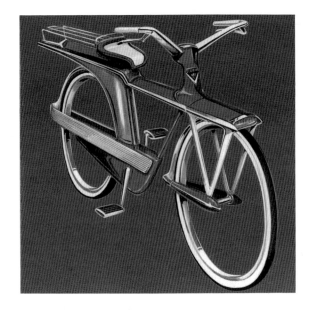

ernment turned a mostly deaf ear to their arguments. Rebuilding Europe, as it turned out, was a priority over rebuilding the old, and sometimes backward, bicycle industry.

The Baby Boom Market

Tariffs were a sore subject for U.S. manufacturers, but the still-growing children's market provided at least one reason for optimism. It was sailing along nicely, due very much to the post-World War II baby boom and to the cleverness of the American makers at designing and selling to the millions of children passing through childhood and into adolescence at the time. This market gained a shot of momentum in 1949 with the introduction of the Schwinn Phantom series, which became an essential status symbol for well-equipped boys. The Black Phantom's (also available in green and red) lines were little different from those of previous balloon-tire models, but the difference in this case was chrome. Chrome fenders, chrome horn tank, and more chrome, wherever a strip of it could be fit, became wildly popular. It was commonly assumed that chrome appealed to youngsters because it reminded them of automobiles and motorcycles, which were having their own love affair with silvery trim at this time as well.

Motor fantasies certainly contributed to bicycle design in the 1950s. Thick tanks were still a standard design feature, as were headlights (sometimes a pair) and, in the case of a popular

PREVIOUS PAGE, RIGHT TOP AND BOTTOM: 1955 Radiobike
Huffman Manufacturing Company, Dayton, Ohio
The radio was the last piece of automobile electrical equipment that was adapted for the bicycle, and it was a natural as long as the bike could accommodate a loop-stick antenna, an on-off lock switch, a battery on the luggage carrier, and a single-tube radio in a moisture-proof, shock-proof, tamper-proof casing in the tank. With the right battery, the radio was typically good for 100 hours. The misfortune of this fine-looking bicycle was that the transistor radio was introduced a year or so later, making this radio seem somewhat obsolete.

Huffman model, a built-in, single-tube radio in the hollow tank and a battery pack behind the seat. The Huffy Radiobike of 1955 demonstrated that Horace Huffy Jr., especially, had his finger on the pulse of what moved kids. He'd remembered his own fascination with radios when he was a child, and what a hit it had made with friends when he'd wired a radio into the family Oldsmobile. The Huffy Radiobike was relatively simple, with thick frame, balloon tires, and upright handlebars. But kids saw it as anything but pedestrian, and it was a big seller for a while, though it was ultimately eclipsed when transistor radios came out a year or two later.

The children's market grew, accounting for the country's second bicycle boom. Three million bicycles were sold in the United States in 1955, reaching that mark for the first time ever.

Besides sheer numbers, there were other similarities to the 1890s' market. Consolidation in the industry took place, much as Albert Pope had attempted at the tail end of his heyday. Now, Huffman Manufacturing successfully expanded by purchasing Monark Silver King, an old company with a relatively new plant in Azusa, California. American Machine and Foundry (A.M.F.) acquired a number of older bicycle makers, including Cleveland Welding, which manufactured Roadmaster models, and opened a state-of-the-art factory in Little Rock, Arkansas. Perhaps most notable among these enormous operations was Murray Ohio Manufacturing, now in Nashville, Tennessee, which acquired the bulk of the contract to produce the Sears Roebuck trademark, J. C. Higgins. Mass retailing, which had confounded the industry in

1950 Hopalong Cassidy Model Rollfast—DPH Products, Cleveland, Ohio
The "Hoppy" was the original "cowboy" bike, of which several followed, but none matched this one for sheer authenticity. Leather holsters, studded guards, horsehair-grain saddle, longhorn handlebars, and "frontier-fringe" carrier were only some of the features. The Rocket Ray fender lamp brought this 24-inch bicycle into the space age at a price that seemed high at $56.95 at the time. Of course many collectors would pay that and more today just for the medallion that came on the tank.

1951 Starlet
Arnold, Schwinn & Co.,
Chicago, Illinois
What Americans wanted in a basic bicycle could not have been more clear. Streamlined, sleek, and sturdy were essential, after which all manner of styling could be applied. The Starlet was luxurious and completely feminine, featuring gorgeous hues such as Holiday Rose, Summer Cloud White, Windswept Green, and Luscious Lavender. There was also the Koroseal saddle and fashionable grips.

NEXT PAGE TOP: 1960
Bowden Spacelander
Bomard Industries,
Grand Haven, Michigan
Perhaps the most unique bicycle of the last fifty years, the Spacelander design was first introduced at London's Victoria and Albert Museum in an exhibition entitled "Designs of the Future" (which also featured an air-conditioned bed). Auto designer Benjamin Bowden conceived it with molded metal which enclosed all moving parts. When it was finally produced by the Michigan company, it was fiberglass and weighted less than 50 pounds. While the design seemed in line with other space-age designs of the period, this one was simply too strange for the conformist period. "Too weird," some kids said, and older ones were on the verge of getting their first three- and ten-speeds anyway. At any rate, only 522 were produced at a price of $89.50. Strangeness and rarity have conspired in recent years to jack the price up to $5,000 and more for a vintage Spacelander in good condition.

the waning days of the first bicycle boom, was returning with a vengeance.

If there was a difference, it was the care with which the makers designed new bicycles for the children's market. Murray even engaged the services of well-known sculptor and industrial designer Viktor Schreckengost to help make critical design changes on a yearly basis. Schreckengost put into words what many people in the bicycle industry already knew: "Children want to imagine an object," he explained in an article in *The American Bicyclist*, "as more than what it is." For years, that image was of motorcycles. But children's fantasies were anything but static.

As balloon-tire riders aged, Schreckengost reasoned, they were exposed to prestigious English "racers," as lightweights were called by youngsters. Typically, they wanted to move up to something lighter, faster, sleeker. This wasn't entirely practical, of course. Children were as

hard on bicycles as dogs on furniture. The problem, and the opportunity, was how to satisfy both children and parents.

The solution was the "middleweight," a cross between the balloon-tire and the racer. Strength was still essential. (Makers developed proprietary welding processes to emphasize the point—"Flash-Welded," from Schwinn, and "Therm-O-Matic," from Columbia.) Now a pair of half-inch tubes might replace a single piece an inch in diameter. Chain guards were not eliminated but reduced in size. Most important, according to the philosophical Schreckengost, was the feature of two-tone color schemes, a sure way to improve the appearance of a bulky machine. And a coat of glossy enamel only added to the fast, light looks.

Unlike the case in the 1890s, the industry's progression of nontechnical design changes—call it planned obsolescence—was an effective

1964 Bowden 300
Febs Industries,
San Francisco, California
Ben Bowden kept trying to get his invention into high-gear production. The 1964 version, the 300, came in a number of colors, including Outer Space Blue, Gold Bronze, Charcoal Black, Fire Engine Red, and Dover Cliff White. A ladies' model was designed but never made. For reasons not unrelated to the original failure, this fine looking bicycle flopped as well, and the fiberglass idea was retired to futurists.

RIGHT AND NEXT PAGE: The strategy of many American manufacturers was to put movie stars on bicycles, both the voluptuous balloon-tire cruiser and fancy lightweight models. Faye Marlow made the point that bicycling had definite European flavor. Actor Buck Jones' point was that a lightweight was an appropriate mount for a cowboy or any American male.

For Health and Pleasure!

1965 Spaceliner
Sears, Roebuck & Co.,
Chicago, Illinois
In the early 1960s, streamlined evolved into "space age," and bicycles were not immune from this styling trend. A national preoccupation with speed and flight saw traditional, sturdy American bicycles go supersonic (at least in looks). The Spaceliner's "jet sweep" tank and slim four-bar frame satisfied the restless earth-bound American youth. Brilliant metallic red added to the effect (turquoise blue for girls). And for a small additional price the Spaceliner came with a Bendix two-speed internal-gear hub a rider back pedaled slightly to shift. Standard tire size on this machine was 26 inches by 1.75 inches—a downsizing from previous popular balloon-tire sizes.

strategy in the 1950s. It was luck, perhaps, but also simple Baby-Boom demographics. This time, bicycles captured a generation when it was young. For the next forty years, that generation would remain hooked, and usher in a series of modern bicycle booms that would have astounded even Victor Schreckengost.

Chapter Eight

The Bicycle Renaissance

AN IMPORTANT EVENT for American bicycles occurred in September 1955, when President Eisenhower suffered his first heart attack. The nation, in the midst of postwar prosperity, was greatly shocked that its vigorous President could have been stricken. The White House was quick to bring in a cardiologist who was not only a leader in his field, but who had the public presence to calm the nation's fears.

The cardiologist was Dr. Paul Dudley White of Boston, a chiseled Yankee with a bushy white mustache. White was not only a leading medical man who explained to the nation that the President would be 100 percent before long, he was a man with another message which he spread with the passion of a zealot. The doctor was a devoted enthusiast of bicycles.

Paul Dudley White had grown up with bicycles. His father was a wheelman during the bicycle boom of the 1890s, and he used to tell his son of early bicycle treks from Boston to Albany, thence to New York City and back to Boston. Young Paul was always excited by these stories and was on a bicycle as soon as he was old enough to ride. It became a standard mode of transportation for him, and by the time he enrolled at Harvard, he commuted to school from his house in Roxbury every day. It was a round trip of ten miles, a distance "which was perfectly easy and practical," White said years later.

White then married, and he and his wife together became enamored of the bicycle. In the

RIGHT: Varsity Eight-Speed; Arnold, Schwinn & Co., Chicago
Racers with derailleur-type gears had been attempted by American manufacturers, including Schwinn, in the 1950s, but without success. By 1960, a Schwinn distributor in California noted that the time had come, and Schwinn started with this eight-speed model. It was not light, rather its frame was closer to a heavy duty cruiser than a lightweight European racing model. But the gearing was like nothing the youth market had seen, and the drop handlebars provided the Varsity with instant visual appeal. It was the beginning stages of a bicycle renaissance that was soon to trickle up to the adult market.

In 1956, Chicago was one of the first major cities to establish a network of bicycle paths through the city's enormous park and forest preserve system. Dr. Paul Dudley White, the famous cardiologist and bicycle promoter, was on hand to help Mayor Richard J. Daley open the paths, and the doctor returned several times to provide support for the effort. On a tandem, Daley (steering) and White seem relatively confident, and the youngsters are obviously comfortable on their bikes. Slightly discomfited by the notion of a two-wheeler is the adult behind Dr. White. Indeed, it was the post-adolescent population that the industry was trying to capture and convert.

early years of their marriage, they made several tours of Europe on the English-style lightweights that they preferred. As he pursued his profession as a heart specialist, White grew increasingly certain of the bicycle's enormous health benefits as well. When he was thrust into the national limelight as physician to America's First Heart Patient, Dr. White finally had the chance to evangelize on the subject. He sometimes lost his audiences, frankly, when he described the medical connection between cycling and circulation. But he looked like a character out of a Norman Rockwell painting (who did indeed make a painting of him), and when translated his meaning was simple enough: A large portion of the heart's inflow of blood came from the legs, and the sustained contraction of leg muscles improved the pumping action of the veins. White also spoke of cycling's calming effect on the nerves, achieved "through improving sleep and maintaining equanimity and sanity."

Within weeks of the Eisenhower heart attack, White had the President on a stationary exercise bike. Within a few months, the result-

ing publicity started an authentic upsurge in cycling among adults. It was a small surge, but enough to counter the quiet resentment toward bicycles that had been held by a portion of the automobile-driving public. In New York City, for example, police unwittingly unloosed a flurry of pro-bicycle publicity when they cracked down on a significant number of bicyclists riding in parks where it was forbidden. Letters to the editors expressed outrage at the wrong-headedness of this policy, especially given the now-well-known health benefits associated with cycling. The result was that the city published a free booklet with a map of the fifty-four miles of bicycling paths that New York City offered at that time.

Chicago was quick to avoid any such embarrassment. In 1956, the city announced the development of thirty-six bicycle paths in parks and forest preserves. To inaugurate the program with appropriate fanfare, Mayor Richard J. Daley invited Paul Dudley White to speak. With all the certainty that an early wheelman might have mustered in the salad days of the L.A.W., White declared that no invention was as noble as the bicycle, and that it was especially edifying for children. A bicycle engendered self-sufficiency, responsibility, and pride, White said. Most of all, he argued, "the bicycle can be presented as another opportunity to learn."

Photographs of the President's heart doctor riding on a tandem with the political boss of Chicago made most people in the bicycle industry smile as broadly as the political entourage watching from the curb. Still, there was work to do to get more people riding bicycles. Ironically, Dr. White's focus on children was representative of a nagging problem within the cycling industry: convincing the public that cycling at its best really was an adult pastime. A number of bicycle executives, including Norman Clarke, president of Columbia, were determined to push that viewpoint harder than ever.

To encourage adult cycling, Columbia in particular became active in sponsoring public bicycle paths in the company's home state of Massachusetts. In 1960, the beginning of the Charles River Basin Bicycle Path in Boston was dedicated and named after native son Paul Dudley White. Another path was opened a year later on Nantucket Island just off Cape Cod. But while these paths were enthusiastically started

with Columbia's money, they were not rapidly finished. Public indifference is always hard to crack, and some people in the industry were at a loss. Clarke remained on the front lines of the cause, however. He believed that political support in high places might help, and he endeavored to do something to attain it.

In 1962, Clarke and other manufacturers of the Bicycle Institute of America (B.I.A.) hosted a Congressional breakfast in Washington. It attracted a number of Senators and Congressmen, as well as members of the Kennedy Administration. At the breakfast, Clarke and other industry leaders thanked the legislators for having curtailed the flood of imports to America with a series of small tariffs over recent years (though the industry was anxious for more.) They also stressed the healthfulness of cycling and argued that riding represented a solution to pollution, recognized as a growing problem at the time.

After the breakfast, Clarke announced that a number of manufacturers had sent bicycles to Washington for the event, and he invited the dignitaries to join him for a ride from the hotel to the Capitol, a distance of a few blocks. A number of them, including Clarke's own Congressman, Silvio Conte, and Secretary of the Interior Stuart Udall, took him up on the offer. It was quite a spectacle. News photographers flocked to the scene.

One outcome of this and related lobbying efforts was a pact with the Department of the Interior that agreed to as much as $2 million in federal funding for bicycle paths—the only requirement being that federal funds be partially matched by the cities and states. Finally, Clarke was seeing progress. Unfortunately, local funding was as stingy as it had been before, and much of the federal money went unspent.

Not entirely daunted, Clarke and the B.F.I. continued to look for answers. They focused on college campuses, which seemed a likely market for the adult lightweights Columbia, Schwinn, and other American companies were now making. But when the manufacturers studied the subject, they found that the average college student thought of bicycles as little more than cheap transportation. Those who owned them mostly owned klunkers. And the professors who rode imports were no role models. "People thought of them as kooks," remembered Clarke years later.

What bicycles needed was a new image. But if a new image was attainable through advertising, it was not something that the industry at large was willing to pay for. A national advertising campaign by the B.I.A. was started in magazines such as *Life,* and then halted after a few months. "Don't tell me about an adult market. There isn't an adult market," the president of another major manufacturer told Clarke.

As it turned out, adults couldn't be told to ride bikes. They had to come to the conclusion themselves. New enthusiasm for cycling did eventually grow, but it was not because of the Bicycle Institute. The renaissance took hold at the grassroots level. Even as bicycle executives were meeting with politicians, a new generation of cyclists, many of them racers, formed in groups around the country. As their successes, and in some cases their lifestyles, became known, these cyclists changed the American consciousness towards bikes.

In 1962, the American bicycle industry needed political support to win tariff protection and generate public enthusiasm for adult riding. Thus, Norman Clarke of the Columbia Manufacturing Company organized a breakfast in Washington D.C. so that the industry could state its case. After breakfast, Dr. Paul Dudley White led a ride to the Capitol, and it was an unexpected pleasure for politicians more accustomed to big black limousines. Leading the way are Secretary of Treasury Douglas Dillon, Dr. White, Congressman Silvio Conte of Massachusetts (to White's left), and Secretary of Interior Stuart Udall.

Pedali Alpini

The sport of bicycle racing had waned during and after World War II, but it had not died. Pockets of enthusiasm remained in the early 1950s. Northern New Jersey, for example, still hosted the 50-mile Tour of Somerville, which survived, if for no other reason than to remember the good old days of bicycle racing in Newark. Kenosha, Wisconsin, had a banked track that was in heavy use; it was considered the oldest continuously used bicycle track in America, and it attracted a hard core of enthusiasts from around the country.

Bob Tetzlaff and George Koenig (behind) were a pair of California riders who took to road racing in the 1950s when ten-speeds were rare in the United States. That did not bother these youngsters who trained hard and started clubs like the Italian-style Pedali Alpini. (Koenig in a green and white Pedali jersey was a founder.) They were among the top riders on a fledgling road racing circuit in Northern and Southern California, and these two made the 1960 Olympic team.

Mostly, the bicycle renaissance—which peaked in the early 70s—got started on the heels of people who had rediscovered cycling on their own. Many became road racers and some even Olympians, but as important as the competition was the fact that there was something beautiful and thrilling about cycling. In an era known for its reaction against social conformity, bicycles separated riders from the mainstream. They could commune with nature. It made them feel slightly European. It was early counterculture.

It grew best, of course, in California, and while cycling flowered anew in many places around the United States, there is something infinitely romantic about the story of cycling in the San Francisco Bay Area, and a group that became known as the Pedali Alpini.

"It will never be as good as it was then," said George Koenig, a founding member of this club and a man whose story comes as close as anyone's to describing the bicycle renaissance. Koenig grew up near the campus of Stanford University, where his father, a German-Jewish refugee, was a professor. As a child George took to bicycles—they were heavily utilized on campus during the gas rationing of the war—and for several years he spent much time hanging around the local bike shop in Palo Alto. In his late teens, Koenig was in the right place at the right time to buy something that was rare at the

time: a French racer, an Automoto with drop handlebars and a four-speed derailleur.

There weren't many people doing this "European" kind of cycling at the time, but the bicycle "underground" quickly led Koenig a few miles south to San Jose, where he found a family of brothers, the Gattos, who were retired racers from the 1930s. The Gattos were hardly similar to Koenig—they were working-class guys who had raced bicycles when it had helped them to scratch together a living in hard times. But they liked George, the professor's son, and often invited him to ride out to the family's walnut-shelling plant outside San Jose. They would tell him stories of what it had been like in the old days. They encouraged him to go to Europe, which he did in 1955. With a friend, Koenig pedaled from Paris to Rome, and at the end of his trip he came back to the states with a new Lazzaretti with chrome lugs and silver paint.

This bicycle was impressive, though mainly to Koenig, because serious cycling was still a mystery to the vast majority of people, even in California. Then, early the next year, Koenig was riding on a quiet road outside Palo Alto when he saw a strange form coming toward him. At first he wasn't certain what it was, but when it whizzed past, he recognized it as another cyclist on a bicycle with turned-down handlebars. Almost simultaneously, both riders circled around. They stopped, and Koenig met Rick Bronson, who was two or three years younger.

Bronson's introduction to bicycles, Koenig learned, had been much like Koenig's. Bronson, too, had wandered into cycling and now was riding mostly by himself. Naturally, the two began riding together, and before many weeks had passed, Bronson insisted that they go to Europe.

That trip, if it did not change the course of American cycling, certainly changed the two riders' lives. Bronson had an introduction to meet the Cinelli family, the famous bicycle makers of Monza, and with the family's help, Bronson and Koenig were entered in a number of junior races in northern and central Italy. After a few months they returned home and instantly started their own club, modeled after clubs they had ridden with in Italy. The Pedali Alpini, or "Alpine Cyclists," they called them-

The 1960 U.S. Olympic team poses in the countryside outside Rome. The road racers on the Olympic team were all from California. In the front row, they were Bob Tetzlaff (second from left), Michael Hiltner (center), George Koenig (second from right), and Lars Zebroski (far right). The track racers were mostly from the Midwest, around one of the only velodromes left in the United States, in Kenosha, Wisconsin. For all of them, Italy was the home of many great heroes of their sport, and even though the Americans came home with no medals, the Rome Olympics represented a solemn pilgrimage.

selves. They sent to Italy for special jerseys—green and white, with a black stripe—and before long they attracted a number of other riders from the southern Bay Area.

The Pedali got increasingly serious, finding road races, some of them quite informal, around California, and often doing well. (Koenig eventually made the Olympic team in 1960.) If all members were single-minded about cycling, none were more so than Bronson. He learned enough Italian to read the cycling journals he received from Italy. He insisted that pasta was the only carbohydrate with sufficient protein to meet his needs. He named his dog Fausto, after Italian cycling great Fausto Coppi, and bewildered his parents completely when he gave up his rock & roll records and started playing opera on his phonograph. The parallels between Bronson and the main character in the movie *Breaking Away* still make other members of Pedali Alpini smile. Ricky Bronson was, after all, well known in the bicycling circles of Los Angeles, where the script for the movie was prepared some twenty years later.

Pedali Alpini were not alone in the Bay Area. A group called the San Francisco Wheelmen was attracting attention in Golden Gate Park, where it had begun by holding races around an old track that ninety years before had been used for high wheelers. One of the younger riders attached to this group was a kid from Berkeley named Peter Rich, who got his start on a coveted Phantom. Rich was mechanically minded early on, and he often occupied himself by taking his bicycle apart and putting it back together. Eventually, he got himself a Raleigh, and inevitably he experimented with the gears, combining a three-speed derailleur with the three-speed, internal-gear Sturmey-Archer hub (and bringing the machine to nine speeds). He fixed a pair of drop handlebars and went looking for races, which he found with a small but growing group of cyclists.

Rich and other young racers naturally congregated in the few bicycle shops in the area

The 1971 Tour of California was the concept of Peter Rich, an ex-racer and owner of a trend-setting bicycle shop, Velo-Sport Cyclery, in Berkeley. Over seventy riders entered the Tour, and they came from Canada, Mexico, and Germany, as well as the U.S. It was the first look that most Americans had of a stage race—with ten stages over a period of eight days. The Tour affirmed that road racing in America was here to stay, though expenses were too much for the organizers of this one, and the hoped-for "annual" event was not repeated a second time.

that understood them. One near Golden Gate Park was owned by an old European racer named Oscar Juner. South on the Peninsula was Cupertino Bicycle Shop, owned by a mechanic named Spence Wolf, who began importing Cinellis when the Pedali talked him into it. These shops were outposts for a growing sport. Bicycling acquired a broader appeal for a number of reasons. Rich, who later opened a large and successful cyclery in Berkeley called Velo-Sports Cyclery, remembers that the arrival of the complete line of Campagnolo components—introduced here in the early 1970s—gave racing bicycles added prestige. The romance of Italy was irresistible to many people. Moreover, there was something rebellious about bicycles.

Shifting Gears

The sales of European bicycles in America at this time were deeply coveted by American makers, who had looked at many different ways of capturing a growing market on lightweights. Derailleur gears were one technical aspect that was tried early on. Derailleurs had been known in this country since the 1940s, when Norman

Clarke of Columbia saw an early magazine article on the idea shortly after the French maker Heuret had perfected it. In fact, Clarke and his engineers built several prototypes with derailleurs, but they could hardly justify going into production at that time. The market in America was not ready.

In the 1950s, Schwinn decided to try derailleurs, ordering 1,000 gear sets from Europe and fitting them on some of Schwinn's lighter-weight frames. The result was an eight-speed racer—two sprockets in front and four in the rear. The models might sell, engineers said, though one problem was that the rider had to reach nearly to the bottom bracket to shift the front sprocket. Perhaps more serious was the fact that few dealers in Schwinn's vast network knew what a derailleur was, and this was still a period when most could hardly match three-speeds against the foreign competition, much less eight. Schwinn built nearly a thousand derailleur bikes, but they did not sell, and the company eventually disassembled most of them and scrapped the offending gears.

Derailleurs were still a bad memory for Schwinn in the early 60s when its Southern Cali-

LEFT: On the 1971 Tour of California, the first American race of its kind ever, there was no shortage of ritual at the end of each day's ride. At the end of Stage Eight, from the old gold-mining town of Camptonville to Squaw Valley, Dave Brink in the yellow leader's jersey is congratulated with flowers, though he lost his lead that day after a punctured tire early on. Augustin Alcantara, in blue, won the stage and by the end of the next day he finished the race as the overall individual winner.

fornia distributor, Harry Wilson Sales, called and asked if the company could produce 500 copies of a 26-inch bicycle with dropped handlebars and racing gears. "They're all over the place here," said Bob Wilson who headed the Los Angeles distributorship. Schwinn executives in Chicago tried to argue that they had been through this, and it had been a disaster. But Wilson insisted, so Schwinn reluctantly ordered a new shipment of derailleurs from Heuret. The company put eight speeds on its "flash-welded" frame bikes—not the lightest on the road, but among the strongest—and Wilson turned out to be right. The models sold very well, and the remarkable "Varsity" soon-to-be-ten-speed was born.

As fitness became *de rigueur* among Americans in the 1960s, racing bicycles became very fashionable indeed. U.S. consumption of new bicycles hit five million in 1964, twice what it had been a decade before, and it continued to grow unabated for another ten years, mostly on the strength of racing bicycles.

Prominent in this bicycle renaissance was the acceptance of women in racing, a sport which, for most of sixty years, had been a male's domain. Now, publicity about women cyclists was rising, and females on bikes with drop handlebars and derailleurs became as much a statement of modern times as bloomers certainly had been in the 1890s. An important milestone in this slice of bicycle history was reached in 1969, when Audrey McElmury of San Diego was one of three women on the U.S. team to compete in the world championships in Brno in the former Czechoslovakia.

The Brno championships drew more attention than usual, in part because they were taking place on the first anniversary of the Soviet invasion of Czechoslovakia. The press covered events closely, especially when local fans cheered heartily for American racers when they passed, and hissed the Russians. McElmury's moment came in the forty-three mile road race, her specialty, which had started in a downpour. Conditions slowed the whole field, but they caused McElmury to fall as she braked in a turn early in the race. But she got up, raced on, and

Orange jerseys were worn by the Velo-Sport Cyclery team, sponsored by race organizer Peter Rich who owned the Berkeley bicycle shop of the same name. Velo-Sport got second place in the overall team standings. The Mexican team won America's first truly international bicycle race in decades.

NEXT PAGE TOP LEFT: If the bicycles don't date the 1971 Tour of California, the automobiles that trailed the riders and carried their gear certainly did. Ford's Pinto was the official car of the race. The Tour of California was a critical success, but it was too expensive to run a second time.

TOP: The scenery between Camptonville and Squaw Valley was often spectacular, but the roads that cut through were frequently primitive. This stage took its toll on several riders, especially the Velo-Sport Cyclery team which suffered at least one puncture, a bad spill, and other misfortunes—though the California team went on to finish a respectable second among teams overall.

BOTTOM: Before the start of the Tour of California, organizer Peter Rich contacted all police authorities through whose jurisdictions the race would pass. Most were cooperative and trailed the pack to discourage disrespectful motorists. Only in Stockton was a highway patrolman inclined to curtail the race—but seventy riders and at least as many team cars were too much for a single state trooper.

what ensued was a terrific drama. Fortunately, the cold air numbed McElmury's severely bruised hip, but water and blood flowed continuously off her arm. An ambulance gave chase to try to stop her and treat her injuries. But she refused to quit. In the end, she won the race by more than a minute over the second place rider. She was the first American to win a world cycling championship since 1912.

For many reasons, a kind of cult-like fascination with bicycle racing began to grow. Its power was revealed again in 1971 in another first, a 685-mile, eight-day stage race called the "Tour of California" (modeled after the Tour de France). Organizer Peter Rich began this massive effort almost naively, by writing the Commissioner of the California Highway Patrol to find out how an event like this could be accomplished. The commissioner wrote back with a mixed message. First, he said that racing any kind of vehicle at all on public thoroughfares was a violation of California state law. Then, somewhat inscrutably, he also enclosed the names and addresses of the eight re-

gional Highway Patrol Commanders who would have to be contacted if anything like this were ever to get off the ground.

Almost miraculously, it did, and a total of seventy riders started out in California's Central Valley and headed west in what was one of the few staged races ever run in the United States. The event was frankly bigger than Rich himself had anticipated. On the first day, as racers pedaled amidst an army of flagmen, and as spectators and crews rode in cars behind the pack, a traffic jam of prodigious proportions accumulated behind the race.

Most people were amused by it all, but near Stockton the race looked like it was about to lock horns with a particular highway patrolman who seemed determined to rope in the situation. This officer whizzed past the race in his car, and when he was well ahead of the pack at the top of a hill, he stopped, flashing lights ablaze. It was a roadblock, and the patrolman's clear intention was to stop the race that he, or one of his superiors, regarded as a public nuisance and even a hazard. Rich saw what was developing and was concerned. But his worried

look turned to a broad smile when he saw what happened next.

The state trooper motioned the first rider to stop. Instead, the leader pedaled right through, as did the second, the third, and all seventy riders in the race. The flagmen and chase vehicles followed, and before the pack was over the hill, the patrolman was back in his car, driving glumly back to headquarters. He could only report that bicyclists seemed to have an attitude about the law. This was not exactly true. What they had was an attitude about cycling, and as the next two decades proved, it was contagious.

1973 Teledyne Titan
Teledyne Linair, Gardena, California
Teledyne Inc. was one of the nation's largest suppliers of space-age tube fittings and high-tech metal assemblies. The company's broad experience in titanium made it natural for them to enter the bicycle market at that critical moment when the Middle East oil embargo was fueling the bicycle renaissance. Teledyne enlisted the support of Barry Harvey of England, a frame builder and road champion who raced successfully on the Titan. Unfortunately, the bicycle was foiled on the market by the smallest detail imaginable. A crimp on a down tube to accommodate the bracket for a shifting lever weakened the whole frame. When they began to break, Teledyne got out of the business posthaste.

Chapter Nine

New Forms Emerge

THE DEVELOPMENT of American bicycles is no linear progression. Bicycle history instead consists of a series of episodes involving good and even visionary mechanics designing machines that for one reason or another either succeeded or failed at capturing public interest—reasons that can be debated endlessly.

What is certain is that some bicycle manufacturers learned how to circumvent the failures. Best among them was the Schwinn Bicycle Company, whose dealer and distributor network grew so successful in the 1950s that it was challenged in the federal courts as a monopoly. The issue at that time was price fixing (for which Schwinn was exonerated), but the real advantage of having loyal franchises throughout the country was the first-hand contact with bicycle riders that local shops provided. This contact had paid off in the development of American-made racing bicycles. In 1963 it was about to pay off again.

Muscle Bikes

One day early in 1963, Schwinn Vice President Al Fritz got a call from one of his representatives in California. "Something goofy" was happening in bike shops all over Los Angeles, he was told. Used 20-inch bikes were pretty much unavailable. Kids were gobbling them up, outfitting them with "banana seats" and "Texas Longhorn" handlebars and riding happily around their neighborhoods.

It sounded strange to Fritz, especially the seat part. A year or two before, the inventor of the banana seat, Robert Per-

RIGHT AND BELOW: 1972 Lemon Peeler Schwinn Bicycle Co., Chicago, Illinois
Of all the Schwinn Sting Rays, the Lemon Peeler and the other Krates were the hottest and the most heavily outfitted for the imaginary drag strip. It had a "mag" sprocket, chrome-plated fenders, stick-shift lever, spring-suspension front fork, and front aluminum drum expander brake. Schwinn called this the "world's most exciting concept in bicycles." It was a great seller, though the true race-worthy machines were coming from much smaller companies with a better understanding of the BMX phenomenon.

1971 Manta Ray
Schwinn Bicycle Co.,
Chicago, Illinois
The Manta Ray wore 24-inch wheels and was built for bigger kids; it foreshadowed the "cruiser" class on BMX tracks. But in Schwinn's mainstream market, riders who might have ridden this one were hankering for ten-speed racers. Thus, the Manta was built for only two years, which makes it rare and very desirable for collectors of the growing muscle-bike category.

sons, whose family business was the oldest saddlemaker in the United States, had tried to interest Schwinn in the long, narrow saddle. Persons suggested that Schwinn use them on tandems, an idea that the bike maker rejected without much thought. But Fritz recalled that he had a few banana seats stored away in the factory, and after finding a set of longhorn handlebars as well, he rigged up one of the California concoctions for himself.

Fritz was always looking for something new for the market, but he did not think too much more about his strange prototype for a while. That was because Frank W. Schwinn, Ignaz' son and the backbone of the company for several decades, was ailing. Schwinn died in

early 1963; his funeral brought all distributors and many dealers to Chicago to pay their respects. It was an emotional and difficult time for everyone at Schwinn, but after the services at Holy Name Cathedral, Fritz invited three of his larger distributors back to the plant. It was closed that day, and Fritz thought it would give them a place to talk. Almost as an afterthought, he brought out the 20-inch banana seater to show his guests.

The distributors were initially unimpressed, but then Fritz took them upstairs to the paint shop, which had wide aisles, and asked each to have a ride. He saw that they were surprised that it was so agile and comfortable. The distributors remained noncommittal, but they were smiling.

1970 Highrise Chopper
Raleigh Company,
Nottingham, England
The American impulse was to create fantasies of a machine that to most Europeans was a practical mode of transportation. Ultimately, the American way was adopted by Raleigh which advertised this five-speed as "the hot one." They went on: "For guys and gals who want a bike built for action. With the lid off! This is a machine with a mind of its own . . ."

A little later, Fritz heard again from his California people. Could he hurry up and get something in production? Already, rumors were that Huffy's Azuza, California, plant was looking at the idea too.

Days later, as Fritz was working out production of this potential new model in his mind, he was carrying prototypes around in the trunk of his car. One morning, president Frank V. Schwinn, Frank W.'s son, noticed him rolling one of the prototypes in from the parking lot. Schwinn asked what it was. Fritz said, "A Sting Ray"—the name had come to him as he sifted through the dictionary for a name that would sound good with Schwinn. Frank V. scoffed mildly, and Fritz said that if he were a gambler he'd bet Schwinn would sell 25,000 of them before the end of the year. What actually happened was that they sold 45,000, and they might have pushed more out the door if they hadn't run into a shortage of 20-inch balloon tires.

The era of the "muscle bike," as this class of bicycles was soon called, was a relatively short one for many bicycle makers, but it was extremely prosperous. High-powered muscle cars such as the GTO, Camaro, Mustang, and Road Runner were the rage among the older set. And with a sleek seat and high-rise handlebars, bike riders could imagine a quarter-mile drag strip on their very own sidewalks.

Elaborate variations on the basic Sting-Ray were soon in the offing. By 1968,

Schwinn held its lead with the Krate series—Orange Krate, Apple Krate, Lemon Peeler, and others. These bikes featured a 16-inch front wheel and a slick-tread 20-incher in back. A

large stick on the cross bar shifted the five speeds.

Huffy entered this market early on as well and had success with the Slingshot, and Raleigh threw off all English reserve and claimed that its Chopper provided "the kind of power and dash normally encountered only on the dragster circuit." In fact, the racy features did nothing for performance and probably slowed the machines down. But that did not prevent AMF from getting Andy Granatelli to endorse their model.

The muscle bike came to an end around 1974 when federal product standards stepped in and tamed the bicycles that caused front headers (with front disk brakes) and back headers (the result of wheel stands) as no bicycle had done since the treacherous high-wheelers of the previous century. But even as one era was ending, another industry that overlapped muscle bike madness was just then on the rise and beginning to take on a life of its own.

Bicycles Meet Motorcross

Once again, California riders were building not just a market for new bikes, but a kind of subculture around them. This was the "Bicycle Moto-Cross" (or BMX) phenomenon—a trend that would ultimately leave the mighty Schwinn company behind. The first recorded race day in BMX history took place in Santa Monica, California, in July of 1969. It was at a place called Palms Park, with a park attendant doing the organizing. Other BMX events followed, often on vacant lots, with teenagers acting as promoters.

Whatever critical mass something new requires, this one had it almost instantly. And it did not take long for adults to notice, and, in some measure, to institutionalize it. In 1971, a motorcycle documentary entitled *On Any Sunday* opened with a sequence of BMX riders sliding against berms and flying over jumps. Southern California kids recognized themselves instantly, and young riders everywhere saw that this was something they could do with available technology. And some fathers—mostly in the California hot bed—started talking to their kids about what kind of bikes worked best.

On this subject, quite a few were specific. Among other changes, the riders said that the

BELOW: In 1974 Linn Kasten was a motorcycle frame-maker who applied his skills to early BMX racers. The company he built was Redline which became one of the major forces in the sport. Kasten's innovations of chrome-molybdenum tubes, forks, and even cranks provided lightness and strength that were unimaginable at the time. Upstarts like Redline—whose 1985 model 600C is pictured here—quickly displaced the large bicycle makers who were much slower to innovate with materials, geometry, and team sponsorship.

OPPOSITE PAGE: In 1974, Yamaha saw the possibility of making it big in BMX. The Japanese company came out with the first full-suspension model, the Moto Bike. Yamaha made major contributions to racing in California in the early days, including the Yamaha Gold Cup series (finals took place in the L.A. Coliseum). Ultimately, however, the real prizes of the industry went to BMX dads like Linn Kasten of Redline and Gary Turner of GT who began by fashioning frames and accessories in their garages.

bikes needed higher bottom brackets and longer cranks (standard Sting Rays came with 4-1/2-inch cranks). A few dads with welding equipment soon came through, with frames not just for their own kids but for their friends as well. This led to the opening of some small enterprises, such as that of Linn Kasten, a custom motorcycle frame maker. By 1974, he was busy producing and selling a line of BMX products called Redline. Also in 1974, the Japanese motorcycle maker Yamaha sensed a chance to establish early brand loyalty. It produced the Moto-Bike, with an impressive-looking rear, twin shock absorbers. The latter feature was not a smashing success in races—riders declared it mushy. But it did lead to "bunny hop-

ping" in which youngsters compressed the shock just before hitting a mogul and used the released energy to launch spectacular leaps.

Knobby tires, banked turns, factory-team jerseys, and high excitement under the lights made BMX racing a sport that was unlike any others. This photo was taken at the Yarnell, California, BMX track in 1977.

Anyone doubting that BMX was more than a fad needed only to follow the Yamaha Gold Cup series. Beginning in 1974, preliminaries were held at Southern California high school football fields (since bleachers were essential).

Finals were at the Los Angeles Coliseum, where fiberglass berms, wooden jumps, and temporary waterholes were placed over the field.

Exposure spawned new BMX manufacturers, and in a very few years, cottage (or garage) industries had grown into empires. Large bicycle makers—ever conservative—were well behind and strained to compete with specialized companies like Redline, GT, Diamond Back, and others, which sponsored teams, paid for their equipment, and entered their riders (few of them over sixteen years old) in actual pro races with prize money that was in the hundreds of dollars.

For the remainder of the 70s and into the 80s, BMX experienced amazing new activity, with new tracks, endless products, several sanctioning bodies, and a few scoundrel-promoters all involved in the growth. The sport reached a climax of sorts in 1984 with a number of important events. First, one of the sport's top riders, a teenager from Riverside, California, named Stu Thomsen, signed a contract with Huffman Manufacturing to race for Team Huffy and put his name on a mass-market special being built and sold by the country's biggest manufacturer. Thomsen's yearly salary was a reported $100,000.

Nineteen eighty-four was also the year that the A.B.A. (American Bicycle Association) Grand Nationals featured one of the most exciting races ever. On an indoor track in Tulsa, Oklahoma, Thomsen and a challenger named Pete Loncarevich went up against each other in the final heat of the pro-class category. Loncarevich crashed on the first jump, and Thomsen went down a moment later in the first turn. Both recovered, caught, and passed the rest of the field. Loncarevich won by several lengths, with blood streaming down his face.

In an equally startling, albeit less bloody, demonstration at the "Grands" that year a kid named Jose Yanez premiered his back flip

In 1984, Huffy came out with a BMX model and named it for one of the greatest professional racers in the sport, Stu Thomsen. Thomsen was one of the biggest names in BMX since 1979 when he emerged as champ of the American Bicycle Association's first season of full-fledged pro racing. Huffy was looking for a way to make a big impact on the BMX market and paid Thomsen a reported $100,000 that year to put his signature on their bike. Unfortunately, the mass marketers could not break through, and the big names in BMX racing continued to be smaller companies like Redline and GT.

Birth of the Mountain Bike

It is the nature of bicycle history to be inflated by myth, a problem that goes clear back to da Vinci's possible conception of the bicycle. Ironically, the problem is worse in history's most recent chapters, as new refinements in the technology and sport have developed simultaneously in different places and for myriad reasons.

Enter the mountain bike, which proved that new bicycle booms were not just possible but could dwarf any that had come before. The advent of the mountain bike cannot be attributed to a single place or event. What is certain is that by the late 1970s there were many forces motivating riders to leave paved roads for greener pastures.

The recognized fathers of mountain biking can say only that it began as a variation on bicycling by people who almost everyone would say were nonconformists. Cycling on bad roads, after all, was precisely what the League of American Wheelmen was founded

Twenty-inch bikes were for small kids exclusively until the bigger ones started racing them at the local BMX track. At Saddleback, in Southern California, the National Bicycle Association Supernationals in 1979 turned out the best of them who decked themselves out in a full complement of protective gear for races.

in a show between races. Yanez had learned the stunt on a homemade ramp that fed into the Salt River in Arizona. At the Grands, his demonstration gave the stamp of official approval to "free-styling" (as if the riders had needed any such an endorsement, for many had been free-styling for years). Perhaps more to the point, it motivated the manufacturers to design and build ever more advanced wheels and frames.

to fight. In more recent years, the expense and delicacy of alloy frames and racing components suggested that only fools would go off the road. ("Cyclo-cross," road racing with some rough spots, had about the same popularity as bicycle polo, which never caught on, despite repeated attempts to churn it in the cycling press.)

As early as the mid-1960s, there were stories of a group of daredevils who found particular charm in pushing old balloon-tire bikes up the mountain roads in Marin County, California, then racing down at speeds that threatened both man and machine. They called themselves the Canyon Gang, after Madrone Canyon on the edge of Mount Tamalpais, the county's highest point. Legend has it that this group held a race in 1969, which would certainly make it the first off-road fat-tire race on record—but the fact was that the Canyon Gang was not particularly competitive.

Their antics might have been lost to history entirely if it weren't for a younger group of cyclists in Marin County who for a variety of reasons noticed what the Canyon Gang was doing. These younger kids were definitely serious about their bicycles, and some of them were hard-core racers. Organized as the Velo Club Tamalpais, they kept their expensive Eu-

ropean machines in perfect tune and rode them some 200 miles a week. Incongruously perhaps, they were attracted to a bunch of older guys who looked like they were trying to beat their bicycles to death.

The best bikes for this purpose, of course, were old cruisers—"curb-slammers"—that were first popular in the 1930s. Whatever it was that the Velo Club liked about these antiques, a few of them became passionate on the subject. Most of the Canyon Gang was retired by the early 70s, but the Velo Club guys found some of their old trails, put good tires on old klunkers, and had more screaming fun than they ever had at a serious road race.

Eventually Velo Club members were sifting through old junk yards for frames. One often-told story of this sort is about Velo Club member Joe Breeze, twenty years old in 1973 when he and a friend were in Santa Cruz. There they found an elderly dealer with a 1937 Schwinn Excelsior which they bought for $5. Breeze took the Excelsior back to the Sausalito bike shop where he worked, fixed it up, and created what was then a state-of-the-art bicycle for riding down the side of a mountain.

Others did the same, mostly with single-gear hubs, new steel rims, and knobby tires. The kids in the Velo Club did not give up their racers, but riding them now seemed like work

ABOVE AND OPPOSITE PAGE BOTTOM: The Repack Race Course in Marin County was established in 1975. It was named because riders claimed a hard run burned all the lubricant out of a good coaster brake, and then you'd have to repack it with new grease. In 1976, Repack drew these fifteen competitors and probably more for one of the many races. Second from left is Wende Cragg, one of the few ladies among the pioneers of mountain biking. Eighth, ninth, and tenth from left are Charlie Kelly, Gary Fisher, and Joe Breeze who were among the earliest entrepreneurs in the mountain bike business. The 1.8-mile course, a relatively flat part of which is shown here, was the site of mountain biking's most important races until 1984 when hikers and other outdoorspeople took issue with the explosive sport.

compared to hitching rides up Mount Tam, ducking under the gates of the fire protection roads, and letting it rip on the way down. For at least two years they explored the area around Mount Tam in this way, enchanted by their new view of the wilderness. Naturally, their attention was also fixed on the bicycles and how they could improve them. Some added braces to the fork blades, as on old Phantoms (though the "knee-action" suspension of that model was a bust on the roughest trails). Others put on motorcycle handlebars. But improvements were basic. Even internal-gear rear hubs were considered too elaborate by most early Marin mountain bikers, who liked to say that this was the "primitive side" of cycling.

An important turning point in the development of mountain bikes came in a series of

was filled with bicycle frames that went back to the 50s, 40s, and even earlier. The farmer had no use for them and said Kelly could take what he wanted. "It was like plundering Rome," Kelly later said. What he could not take he remembered, and a few weeks later he sent his roommate, Gary Fisher, another road racer, to go have a look for himself.

The best frame Fisher came back with would have a role in one of the biggest revolutions in bicycles of the 20th century. It was a 1934 Schwinn—also an Excelsior—strong, fil-

BELOW: The 1937 Schwinn Excelsior that Joe Breeze found in a Santa Cruz bike shop was minimally outfitted for off-road mountain racing. There was an initial reluctance to apply fancy components; Breeze liked to talk about the "primitive side" of bicycling. Still, the strength of the old Schwinn and its high clearance between the hanger bracket and the ground made this an ideal frame for the most rigorous downhill racing.

RIGHT: Joe Breeze on the hellish Turn No. 4 on Repack in 1977. He holds the record for the most wins on the course which was relatively abandoned in 1984 after the politics of hikers, and the many jurisdictions in charge of the trails made it necessary to find remoter climes for mountain biking.

events in 1974. Charlie Kelly, one of the Club's stalwarts, made a living as a road-crew member for a Northern California rock band, Sons of Champlin, and as he drove the band's truck up and down the state, he sought out bicycle graveyards where he might find the kind of frames that he and his friends coveted. One evening, while driving along Interstate 5, he was led to one of the greatest junk piles he'd ever seen, at an old farm outside Redding. It

let-brazed, and just about as basic a bicycle as was ever made. It was rusty, but the heavy tubing could be easily cleaned. Best of all, the '34 had a good two inches more clearance than most cruisers had between bottom bracket and the ground. This, Fisher already knew, would be important for riding over rocks and logs. It also enabled him to put on slightly longer cranks.

Purists among Club Velo members were not all in favor of Fisher's next alteration—a five-speed derailleur on the rear hub. But it seemed to work. Then Fisher found a used drum brake from a heavy old English-made tandem which was strong and also kept the brakes dry when fording puddles and shallow streams. These and a few other refinements, some said, were too sophisticated for the mountain. But they all admitted that Gary Fisher's "ballooner" was about as high-performance as you could get.

All of which made the next step inevitable. As soon as the Velo Club had found a suitable place they began racing their klunkers. That place turned out to be an old trail that they found on Pine Mountain just north of Mount Tam, and in 1976 they rigged up some primitive timing equipment by synchronizing a navy chronometer at the top of the mountain with an alarm clock at the bottom. At the first race, the club sent a dozen racers down the 2.2-mile course at two-minute intervals. A San Francisco fireman named Joe Burrowes won with an unrecorded time.

In the weeks and years that followed, many other riders who had also begun riding mountain trails elsewhere in the Bay Area found out about the organized races and showed up at the course that had become known as "Repack." (The name was coined when someone noted that you had to repack your coaster brake with new grease after every hard run.) As competition increased, it was evident that anyone who could break five minutes on Repack was doing well. Fisher, on his Schwinn, set a 4:22 record in 1976 that still stands in record books now faithfully preserved by riders who are now in middle age.

With racing times measured in seconds, the next inevitable step was to devise better bikes that would go faster. Eschewing the "primitive side," a number of riders worked on new frames. Among them was the former purist Joe Breeze, whose father was an engineer and a former road racer himself. Using his 1937 Excelsior as a model, Breeze tirelessly worked out the geometry of the ideal frame before ever cutting tube. His result had the look of an old cruiser, but because the frame was of chrome-molybdenum it weighed about 20 pounds, less than half of what an old one had weighed.

Charlie Kelly was a roadie for a rock-and-roll band and later was partner with Gary Fisher in the first MountainBikes shop in San Anselmo, California. But nothing pleased him like packing his bike—which was becoming increasingly more sophisticated—and riding through the wilderness. This photo was taken in Mineral King National Park, California, in 1978. The bicycle is an early high-performance machine.

"Town Bike," now on display in the Mountain Bike Hall of Fame and Museum, has knobby tires, basket, mud guards, and a neglected paint job, all essential features of a type of machine that served as transportation and reverse status symbol in Crested Butte, once the alter ego of neighboring Aspen, Colorado, and a cradle of mountain bikes in the 1970s.

An industry was being born. Around this same time—accounts vary as to whether it was in 1976 or 1977—a Palo Alto frame builder named Tom Ritchey started talking to Joe Breeze about high-performance klunkers. Eventually, Ritchey built one for Fisher, who outfitted it with expensive components. Ritchie built nine more, and when he couldn't sell them immediately, he let Fisher and Kelly try peddling them out of the back of their car. It was ambitious stuff for a couple of "wild-eyed hippies," as Kelly admitted. But they collected $1,200 on faith from their first few buy-

ers, then went out to buy components. It was a strange business, but Fisher and Kelly were soon successful enough to open a storefront garage in the nearby town of San Anselmo. Their company, MountainBikes, grew, though it outgrew the partnership. (Sadly, Fisher and Kelly failed to license their trade name.)

Predictably, off-road cycling was being invented in other places as well, and nothing made the Bay Area riders happier than to find compatriots. Another cradle of mountain biking turned out to be in the real mountains: in Crested Butte, Colorado, which also lays claim

to the early evolution of the sport. In 1976, the story goes, a group of firemen from the town tried a feat they had talked about for a long time: riding across Pearl Pass from Crested Butte to Aspen, 40 miles and 12,000 feet at the highest point.

This ride drew notice in the *Co-Evolution Quarterly* (a descendant of the *Whole Earth Catalogue)*. Naturally, the Californians made contact immediately, and many made plans to go out and try the Pearl Pass run themselves. Unfortunately, the second annual event was canceled, as the Colorado riders were busy fighting forest fires after a dry summer. But the next year, in September 1978, the Marin group traveled to Crested Butte, where the natives were definitely impressed by the Californians' fancy bicycles. To the visitors, the Buttians' lack of technology made their pedaling all the more impressive. *Outside* magazine found them all interesting, did a story, and the publicity that was generated thereafter created an industry.

Actually, it was as if a new and innovative industry was superimposed on an old, conservative one. Mountain bike designers had plenty of ideas, which they executed as best they could, although many of the parts and components that they might have preferred simply weren't

Doug "The Bump" Ayrud goes over a modest jump on his klunker at the first Fat-Tire Festival in Crested Butte, Colorado, in 1976. "Buttians" had long made use of cruiser bikes to get around town, and some of the stronger bodies went off road and into the mountains. But formal competition, however tongue-in-cheek, was never organized until the winter of 1976 when there was no snow, no skiing, and plenty of time on everyone's hands. Events moved quickly for these proto-mountain bikers. Today, Crested Butte is the home of the Mountain Bike Hall of Fame and Museum.

available. It took the industry standard-bearers a while to catch on. Only by 1979 did parts manufacturers finally think to make aluminum rims and high-quality tires in the 2.125-inch size that mountain bikers required. (In fact, it was the cruiser-class BMX bicycle, not mountain bikes, that ushered in this improvement.

Little by little, Breeze, Fisher, and several others were building bicycles that they were starting to call "user-friendly" because they were more comfortable than anything else on the market at the time. But even by the end of the 1970s their output was small—maybe a dozen bikes a month among them—and their prices were still very high.

PREVIOUS PAGE TOP AND BOTTOM: In 1976, some wealthy Aspenites crossed Pearl Pass on their big, loud dirt bikes and rolled into quiet Crested Butte, reportedly, for drinking and carousing. Later that summer, members of the Crested Butte Hot Shot forest fire crew returned the "favor" by making the same 42-mile trip to Aspen on their single-speed klunkers, where they showed that they could not only ride bicycles over hard terrain, but could drink and carouse in Aspen as well as anyone. Reports of the first Pearl Pass Tour were published in the Co-evolution Quarterly and caught the attention of mountain bikers in Marin County. They resolved to make the second Pearl Pass tour (which came in 1978 since fires kept the Buttian riders busy in 1977). These photos document the second Pearl Pass Tour, with Albert Maunz, Bob Starr, and Jim Cloud pushing their bikes near the summit of the 12,700-foot pass. In the group photo Wende Cragg is at left, Charlie Kelly is fourth from left, Joe Breeze is fifth from left, and Gary Fisher is third from right.

TOP: Breezer Number One was the first of mountain-bike pioneer Joe Breeze's ten original frames, built in 1976 for speed and durability on the mountain. Breeze, a road racer who found new thrills on rough, steep trails, had little precedent for this design, but he was inspired by the old cruisers, mostly Schwinns, that were viewed as the most dirt-worth bicycles up until that time. Early Breezes featured chrome-moly tubing and twin laterals which reduced flex and breakage under conditions that tested any bicycle. The top tube slopes forward for reasons of rider clearance and to accommodate the only seat tube available at that time.

A small California company, Specialized Bicycle Components, made the first move toward mass-production. In 1981, they got frames from Japan and came on the market with Stumpjumpers, selling about 1,200 copies in a year. Ben Lawee, a Southern California marketing guru, followed suit and sold 1,800 Univega mountain bikes in 1981 as well. What followed was a modern-day bicycle boom, the likes of which no one had ever seen before. Sales kept tripling for a decade, and by 1993, 8.4 million mountain bikes were sold. It was more than 95 percent of the total U.S. market.

Quite obviously, mountain bikes breathed new life into the bicycle market. What was less obvious was the direction of technical development, which was accomplished, as bicycle technology always has been, in spurts and starts. Gary Fisher, whse company was now called Fisher Mountain Bikes, had to put up what was for him a huge letter of credit to have a new-style fork manufactured in Japan. (The Unicrown fork was a cross between a BMX and a road fork.) New cantilever brakes had to be developed, as Fisher, Breeze, and others searched for something that would give the service of a drum brake but not sacrifice a high-quality front hub. Ultimately, new and stronger headsets were also developed but this not until 1989 when the industry—still standard-bound—finally moved to adopt a steering system that was as strong as the rest of a typical mountain bike.

Experimentation accelerated, naturally, with the volume of sales. Index shifters were developed to click, rather than slide, into a gear change. New frames and radical geometries were devised in a quest for the lightest and most dirt-worthy designs possible. Racing teams were assembled to promote brand names and to develop increasingly sophisticated equipment. A racer name Paul Turner invented a front fork with two small hydraulic cylinders for effective front end suspension. They were called Rock Shox.

It all led to an industry of formerly small companies such as Specialized and Trek (which absorbed Gary Fisher's company) that grew large on the strength of mountain bikes. The irony, of course, is that mountain bike technology, once slow in evolving, is now pervasive and perhaps overused; millions of bicy-

1995 Klein Mantra
Klein Bicycle Corporation,
Chehalis, Washington
It was called (by its makers) the
"optimum cross-country suspension
bicycle." The main, and most
esoteric, feature of this bicycle is
frame geometry that places the
rear suspension pivot at such a
location that the shock is only
activated when it is desirable. The
frame weights only 4.8 pounds, a
figure inversely proportionate to
the its $4,000 price (frame only).

1995 Sport Touring #1250 Waterford Precision Cycles, Waterford, Wisconsin The Waterford company was created in 1993 by the great grandsons of Ignaz Schwinn who had recently sold the family company to Scott International. Waterford's objective was to build a good, comfortable touring bicycle with tried-and-true geometry going all the way back to the 1938 Paramount. Also similar to the old days, this $1,200 frame was designed to be sold separately, with the serious cyclist buying and applying the desired components.

cles that never leave the pavement are outfitted for hard riding in the mountains. This is the result of the bicycle industry's oldest character trait: single-mindedness. In the mid-1990s, development of ever-better frames and components continued apace. Prices rose to fantastic levels. And as new carbon fiber frames were developed and placed on the market, the business was massaged by the addition of mountain bike racing as a medal sport for the 1996 Summer Olympics in Atlanta.

All of which pleases mountain bike pioneers no end. People who started on confirmed klunkers are now known as technical gurus and household names among millions of enthusiasts. But Joe Breeze, for one, has not been entirely satisfied. After several years of running his own company, then selling it, and then going into business with another manufacturing company, he believed that the true beauty of mountain bikes was being neglected. That was the idea of the bicycle as transportation.

This has brought Breeze full circle. By 1995 he was busy designing a "town bike" that his Japanese backers—a company called Interjet—did not trust at first. They believed racing was the leading edge. Breeze countered that comfort was. The result became a design for a chrome-moly cruiser called the Breezer Ignaz X, homage to the old Schwinns that started the mountain bike craze. The Ignaz X is lighter than the old Excelsior—about 30 pounds instead of 50—and it has a new Shimano three-speed internal-gear hub. It uses the latest welding technology, and its bearings are made to a standard inconceivable in the 1930s. But it has big handlebars and a chain guard. Its keynote is comfort, which Breeze believes was the real reason the mountain bike took off in the beginning.

Sit Back and Ride

As the stories of the BMX and mountain bikes demonstrate, changes in popular bicycles often take place by chance. Major steps forward often occur thanks to disproportionate efforts by individuals or small groups. Their innovations are then widely adopted for reasons that have less to do with the logic of the machine than the collective taste of millions of riders. The converse can also be true: Lack of broad acceptance in the face of mechanical logic is the bane of the "recumbent" bicycle.

Index

Fig.1.

Inventor: